America, We Call Your Name

America,
We Call Your Name

Poems of Resistance and Resilience

Selected by Sixteen Rivers Press

SIXTEEN RIVERS PRESS

Published by Sixteen Rivers Press
P.O. Box 640663
San Francisco, CA 94164-0063
www.sixteenrivers.org

Library of Congress Control Number: 2018947711
ISBN: 978-1-939639-16-5

Design by Josef Beery

The members of Sixteen Rivers Press would like to thank everyone who helped with the creation of this book, especially those who allowed us to use their poems and those who brought other people's work to our attention. We extend our deep gratitude to Ken Haas, who helped us to conceive of this project, and whose vision and support were critical to its realization. And for responding to our request for a foreword with such intelligence and energy, we thank Camille T. Dungy, a true friend of the press, whose own work as poet, essayist, and activist provides a strong model of resistance and resilience.

Within the press, an anthology committee took on this project and saw it through from beginning to end: assistant editors Gerald Fleming, Lynne Knight, Carolyn Miller, Jeanne Wagner, and Helen Wickes, and senior editor Murray Silverstein.

Finally, we would like to thank the friends of Sixteen Rivers Press, our donors, subscribers, and readers; without them, this book, and the press itself, would not exist.

O, yes,
I say it plain,
America never was America to me,
And yet I swear this oath—
America will be!

> —Langston Hughes
> *"Let America Be America Again"*

All I have is a voice
To undo the folded lie

> —W. H. Auden
> *"September 1, 1939"*

Contents

Foreword by Camille T. Dungy   *xiii*

Introduction by Murray Silverstein   *xv*

What Kind of Times Are These

Adrienne Rich, *What Kind of Times Are These*   3

Ada Limón, *A New National Anthem*   4

Brenda Hillman, *Short Anthem for the General Strike*   5

Alison Luterman, *What We Did in the Resistance (Part 1)*   6

John Milton, SONNET XXII: *On the Detraction Which Followed Upon My Writing Certain Treatises*   8

Grace McNally, *Antigone Marches on Washington*   9

Camille T. Dungy, *What I know I cannot say*   10

Miriam Bird Greenberg, *Spirit Level*   12

David Beckman, *my soon-to-be-written protest poem*   13

Heather Bourbeau, *Where the Deer Find Refuge*   14

Leonard Nathan, *Ode*   15

Susan Cohen, *Love in a Year of Outrage*   16

Hard Winter

Frank Bidart, *Mourning What We Thought We Were*   19

Chiyuma Elliott, *I imagined all the place names as code*   21

William Matthews, *A Poetry Reading at West Point*   22

Shu Ting, *Perhaps*   23

Naomi Shihab Nye, *Gate A-4*   24

Matt Daly, *Hard Winter*   26

Judy Halebsky, *Alternative Facts*   27

Martin Ott, *Why We Believe Obvious Untruths*   28

Tania Pryputniewicz, *An Iris for Hillary, January 20, 2017: A Cento*   29

Pablo Neruda, *The great tablecloth*   30

Seamus Heaney, *From the Republic of Conscience*   32

Bonnie Rae Walker, *A Phoenix Flag*   34

The End and the Beginning

Juan Felipe Herrera, *War Voyeurs*   37

Joseph Zaccardi, *The Ones Without Names*   39

Susan Griffin, *Song*   40

Ocean Vuong, *Aubade with Burning City*   42

Yusef Komunyakaa, *Thanks*   44

Carol Dine, *Mother, Flying*   46

Martin Russell, *Rabbit*   47

Dana Koster, *Black Powder*   48

Mona Nicole Sfeir, *Z.*   50

Robert Hass, *Winged and Acid Dark*   51

Natalie Diaz, *Why I Don't Mention Flowers . . .*   52

Dawn McGuire, *American Dream with Exit Wound*   54

Molly Giles, *Letter to My Country in Wartime*   56

Wisława Szymborska, *The End and the Beginning*   57

Laura Da', *American Towns*   59

Gerald Stern, *The Dancing*   62

Jose A. Alcantara, *Violaceae*   63

Jubilee Blues

Claudia Rankine, *because white men can't*   67

Danez Smith, *dear white america*   68

Reginald Dwayne Betts, *When I Think of Tamir Rice While Driving*   70

Forrest Hamer, *Repetition Compulsion*   73

Evie Shockley, *ode to my blackness*   74

Sharon Olds, *Ode to My Whiteness*   75

Terrance Hayes, *American Sonnet for My Past and Future Assassin*   76

Ann DeVilbiss, *Conjure Fire*   77

William Shakespeare, from *The Tempest*, Act I, Scene ii   78

Robin Coste Lewis, from *Voyage of the Sable Venus*, Catalog 4   *79*

Shane McCrae, *America Gives Its Blackness Back to Me*   *80*

Solmaz Sharif, *Mess Hall*   *81*

Tyehimba Jess, *Jubilee Blues*   *82*   ⸺

Robert Hayden, *Frederick Douglass*   *83*   ⸺

The Fool's Song

Anita Sullivan, *Another Reason*   *87*   ⸺

Po Chü-i, *On Setting a Migrant Goose Free*   *88*

W. S. Merwin, *A Message to Po Chü-i*   *89*

Adam Tavel, *The Pillory and the Steepled Dark*   *90*

William Carlos Williams, *The Fool's Song*   *91*   ⸺

Ellery Akers, *April 24, 2017: Reading the News*   *92*

Tomaž Šalamun, *The Right of the Strong*   *93*

Gail Newman, *Earth Day*   *94*

Elizabeth Spencer Spragins, *At Standing Rock*   *95*   ⸺

Meryl Natchez, *why humans?*   *96*

C. P. Cavafy, *The City*   *97*   ⸺

Robinson Jeffers, *Shine, Perishing Republic*   *98*

Molly Fisk, *National Politics*   *99*

Matthew Zapruder, *Sun Bear*   *100*

These Strangers in a Foreign World

Emily Dickinson, *No. 1096* [These Strangers, in a foreign World]   *105*   ⸺ ⸙

Virgil, *The Departure from Fallen Troy*   *106*   ⸺

Mai Der Vang, *Dear Exile*   *107*

Philip Levine, *The Mercy*   *108*   ⸺ ⸙

Diya Abdo, *Blad*   *110*   ⸺

Irma Pineda, *The Baggage*   *111*   ⸺

Dante Alighieri, "*You shall leave behind all you most dearly love*"   *112*   ⸺

Emma Lazarus, *The New Colossus*   *113*   ⸺   ⭒

Anonymous, *That Damned Fence*   *114*

Jaan Kaplinski, "*The East-West border . . .*"   *115*   ⸺

Eliot Schain, *Disciple*   116

Christopher Rubio-Goldsmith, *Growing Up a Halfie*   117 ———

Mahmoud Darwish, *Another Damascus in Damascus*   118

Susanna Lang, *Executive Order*   119

Home to Roost

Jane Mead, *Money*   123

William Blake, *London*   124

Liam Rector, *About the Money*   125

Susan Terris, *GOMER*   127

Janet Jennings, *An Augury*   128

Thomas Centolella, *Ballad of the Indivisible*   129

Ursula K. Le Guin, *American Wars*   130 ———

Rick Barot, *Coast Starlight*   131

Susan G. Duncan, *Kara Walker's Sphinx*   132

Audre Lorde, *When the Saints Come Marching In*   133

William Butler Yeats, *The Second Coming*   134 ———

Kay Ryan, *Home to Roost*   135 ———

Tu Fu, *Jade Flower Palace*   136 ———

America, I Do Not Call Your Name Without Hope

Peter Dale Scott, from "Changing North America"   139

Walt Whitman, "*I resist anything better than my own diversity*"   140

Lucille Clifton, *won't you celebrate with me*   141

Elizabeth Alexander, *One week later in the strange*   142 ———

Ellen Bass, *Ode to the Heart*   143

Dan Bellm, *The Crossing*   144

Tim Vincent, *I Like It When We Sit in the Backyard*   145

George Perreault, *Veterans Day*   146

Austin Smith, *We Defy Augury*   147

Lucille Lang Day, *Inauguration Day in the Galápagos*   148

Julia B. Levine, *Ordinary Psalm with a Four-Letter Word*   149

Percy Bysshe Shelley, *England in 1819*   150

Bei Dao, *The Morning's Story*   151
Patrick Daly, *Chosen*   152
Dean Rader, *"America, I Do Not Call Your Name Without Hope"*   154

Make a Law So That the Spine Remembers Wings

Czeslaw Milosz, *Incantation*   157
Dante Di Stefano, *45th Psalm*   158
Tony Hoagland, *Gorgon*   160
Michael Benedikt, *The Thermometer and the Future*   161
Chana Bloch, *Death March, 1945*   162
Jen Stewart Fueston, *To the Women Marching, from a Mother at Home*   163
Larry Levis, *Make a Law So That the Spine Remembers Wings*   164
Jericho Brown, *The Tradition*   165
Jack Millson, *The Chrysalis*   166
Jocelyn Casey-Whiteman, *Poem for the Future*   167
Joshua Bennett, *America Will Be*   168
Tomas Tranströmer, *Allegro*   170
Prartho Sereno, *When They Arrive*   171
Charles Wright, *Sunlight Bets on the Come*   172
Lisel Mueller, *The Laughter of Women*   173
Jane Hirshfield, *Let Them Not Say*   174

Notes on the Poems   177
Contributors' Notes   181
Permissions   193
Index of First Lines   199
Author Index   202

Foreword
Some Definitions and a Celebration

A watershed maps a region via the waters that flow into and through the area, all heading to a common destination. Watersheds can be huge. We might demarcate the three watersheds of the United States as those waters that flow toward the Atlantic, those that flow toward the Pacific, and those that flow toward the Gulf. Perhaps, on a similarly grand scale, we might say that all our watersheds are connected to the one world ocean. In this way, all of us are connected to the same source and destination. Watersheds can, of course, also be more localized. It is in this localized manner that we tend to best understand the concept of the watershed. Feeding San Francisco Bay are the sixteen rivers from which the press that has published the book in your hands chose its name. These sixteen rivers are fed by countless creeks and streams, some of which assert themselves only on occasion, as is the case with the stream that sometimes muddies San Francisco's Dolores Park or the creek that might course down your sidewalk after heavy rains. These brooks and becks and rivulets, small as they might at first appear, have in them the potential to feed a mighty sea.

In many communities today, a movement is afoot whose mission is to restore and revitalize creeks along their natural courses. We call it *daylighting*, the British call it *deculverting*. This movement holds as its primary concerns land use, access, and power. It is, therefore, wildly contentious. I was recently reminded by the poet Robert Hass that there is a saying in California that all water eventually leads to politics. This is why I started thinking of the San Francisco Bay Area's watersheds as I read the poems collected in this anthology, even though the word *watershed* never appears in the poems and a search of the document produced the word *water* only twenty-eight times. Water, poetry, politics—in some communities, like the one in California where this book was first collected, these three concerns are points of conversation as common as real estate, elections, and traffic. They get all mixed up—by poets and other people—these elemental conversations about water, land, and sky, and the other equally frequent and necessary conversations about who runs the world and how and why.

Hydro engineering is a necessity for the continuation of life as we know it. Dams. Aqueducts. Diverted rivers. Salmon ladders. Flooded rice paddies. Irrigated almond groves. Pool water, lawn water, field water, tap water, bathwater, rainwater, drought. In one of this anthology's poems, a poem called "Money," Jane Mead imagines what might be made possible if less water were diverted from its natural watershed. The poem acknowledges why such a vision could not be fulfilled. "The water didn't belong to the water." Even still, there are people—have always been people—who are looking for new ways we might send the waters on which we rely back along their life-enriching courses. Ways to give the water back to the water. Ways we might, in the process, refresh ourselves.

Another way we think of the word *watershed* is in terms of a watershed moment: a defining moment that changes the direction of a culture, a movement, or a set of ideals. The presidential election of 2016 was such a watershed moment, revealing a political reality that for many had run underground like one of those overlooked streams. The attack on the World Trade Center and the Pentagon on September 11, 2001, that was a watershed moment. It ushered our nation into decades of perpetual war and, as a result, has delivered into our communities surplus and residual byproducts of war in the form of military vehicles used by local police forces, weapons used by citizens against themselves, physically and emotionally traumatized veterans, refugees, and immigrants. All of these complicate our understandings of who we are and who we might become. Though they were here all along, like the muddy waters that rise during the rainy season in Dolores Park, the domestic hostilities accompanying the daylighting of these cultural streams cause us to be more mindful of where and how we

step. Certain watershed moments call us to attention. Poetry also calls us to attention. Poetry helps us understand, more clearly, more articulately, who we are and what we need to be.

There is nothing new about any of this. Politics, water—these have been with humans from the start. And resistance, in humans, must be as natural as resistance in a stream. So we find in this collection poems written out of the confusion and rage in response to the Environmental Protection Agency Secretary's April 2017 announcement of this country's exit from the Paris Climate Accord alongside poems written against the legacy of the 1975 fall of Saigon, a meditation on the Shawnee experience on this continent in 1783, the eighth-century musings of Tu Fu, and Virgil's *Aeneid*. These poets have an urgent message to share with you. This message is brand new, and it is also eternal. Read carefully. What you learn here might just save your life.

A watershed defines the direction of the flow of a sustaining force. Here, we will call that force water—though in other applications we might be understood to be speaking of cultures, visions, ideals. Unless they are diverted—and, for as long as we have been writing, we have been in conversation with the minds that have engineered such diversions—even the smallest streams within a watershed will head toward a common destination. Even if they are initially diverted, many, many streams will eventually head toward a common destination. The waters will be gathered, as these poems have been gathered. Together they will form a mighty body—like the world's one ocean—one it will be impossible to constrain.

—*Camille T. Dungy*
Colorado Springs, March 2018

Introduction

Stunned by the outcome of the 2016 presidential election, three poets met in San Francisco a few days after the election and wondered what poetry might have to say, to and about America, at this moment in our political and cultural lives.

Democracy in America has always been a fragile, imperfect affair, but one that provided an aspirational ideal, a potential yet to be realized, by which a diverse people might yet come to rule themselves, balancing conflicting claims for freedom, equality, and justice. Now, this American idea, this hope, was in jeopardy. The new president quickly turned against the free press, calling it an "enemy of the people." Free speech itself—the first law of poetry—felt suddenly threatened by an authoritarian regime, one whose leader held little regard for the truth.

What were we in for? And what did poetry have to say?

In 2010, Sixteen Rivers Press published an anthology exploring the concept of place in Northern California: *The Place That Inhabits Us: Poems of the San Francisco Bay Watershed*. We gathered poems from a variety of voices, traditions, and subcultures, and we organized the book around the conversations they inspired, finding in them a kind of choral power, a multivoiced song of our region, its history, its sorrows, its treasures, its hopes.

We wondered if something similar could be accomplished on a national scale in response to the election and at this moment in our politics. With our common culture so fractured, what did poetry have to say?

And so we embarked on this anthology in November 2016, under the banner "poems of resistance and resilience." Looking for a diverse, representative blend of voices, we gathered the poems in two ways. First, early in 2017, we conducted a nationally advertised call for submissions, seeking unpublished poems that would "respond to the cultural, moral, and political rifts that now divide our country: poems of resistance and resilience, witness and vision, that embody what it means to be a citizen in a time when our democracy is threatened." We encouraged poets to interpret this call broadly, adding, "We welcome voices raised in passion and in praise, whether lyrical, philosophical, visionary, or personal." In a matter of weeks, we received over two thousand poems from poets writing in response to our call. The work came from across the country, from red states and blue states, high schools and nursing homes, big cities and small towns.

At the same time, we asked members of Sixteen Rivers Press (a shared-work collective of Northern California poets) to nominate poems. These poems could be old or new, published or not, the poets living or dead—work from anywhere that spoke to this moment in the voice of poetry. In this way, we gathered another three hundred poems, ranging from Virgil and Dante to Claudia Rankine and Mai Der Vang, from Milton to Merwin, from Po Chü-i to last Thursday's just-posted Poem-a-Day.

Looking for a 50/50 blend of these two sources, a group of us (Jerry Fleming, Lynne Knight, Jeanne Wagner, Helen Wickes, and myself) began sifting through the poems. Building on the experience of our first anthology, we looked for the ways they spoke to the moment and to each other: challenging, rebutting, affirming, enlarging. Gradually, the nine sections of the book emerged, each a kind of town-hall meeting of citizen-poets gathered to raise their voices, now raucous, now muted, now lyric, now plain: voices responding with dissent and consoling with praise, perspective, vision, and hope.

The first two sections cope with the days that followed the election; some poems saying, "I thought we were better," some, "It's just as we feared," they make their way through the confusions of American life in the winter and spring of 2016 and 2017.

The five sections at the center of the book speak to our deeper troubles as a country: violence, misogyny, racism, ecocide, xenophobia, economic injustice—hard truths, but not the whole truth. In the middle of the section on war, for example, we find Robert Hass quoting Bashō: "If the horror of the world were the truth of the world, / . . . there would be no one to say it / and no one to say it to." Poetry may sometimes reflect the horror of the world, but it also gives voice to the possibilities for greatness embodied in human existence. And what it sees and loves it wants to praise, as in the poems of our last two sections.

Czeslaw Milosz opens the final section with these lines: "Human reason is beautiful and invincible. / No bars, no barbed wire, no pulping of books, / No sentence of banishment can prevail against it." He is writing in Berkeley in 1968, with the country in shambles—the assassinations, Viet Nam, riots in the streets. The poem is titled "Incantation," words used to invoke a magic spell. In the face of moral collapse, poetry says, words can use their magic to name and value truth. This struggle is young and beautiful, Milosz tells us, and poetry is its "ally in the service of the good." Resistance breeds resilience breeds resistance.

The last poem in the book, Jane Hirshfield's "Let Them Not Say," appeared online on January 20, 2017, Trump's Inauguration Day, as the Academy of American Poets' *Poem-a-Day*. "Let them not say," writes Hirshfield, "it was not spoken, not written. / We spoke, / we witnessed with voices and hands."

Around 1950, Pablo Neruda wrote the poem "América, I do not call your name without hope" to a Latin America in crisis. Translated by Robert Bly, the poem found a life in English: "America. . . . I sleep and awake in your fundamental sunrise: / as mild as the grapes, and as terrible, / carrier of sugar and the whip. . . ." In this anthology, Dean Rader's poem, in the spirit of Neruda's but in the time of Trump, speaks, under the same title, to our America, "This is for you and your fear, your tar, / for the white heat in your skin and / for your blue bones that one day may sing." Our title echoes this cry: America, listen to what your poets are saying. Are we the corrosive, racist, authoritarian regime that the 2016 election brought to power, or are we a democracy, that fragile, imperfect form of government that must be constantly guarded in the struggle for equality and freedom? In resistance and resilience, and not without hope, America, we call your name.

—*Murray Silverstein*
Oakland, March 2018

What Kind of Times Are These

What Kind of Times Are These

There's a place between two stands of trees where the grass grows
        uphill
and the old revolutionary road breaks off into shadows
near a meeting-house abandoned by the persecuted
who disappeared into those shadows.

I've walked there picking mushrooms at the edge of dread, but
        don't be fooled,
this isn't a Russian poem, this is not somewhere else but here,
our country moving closer to its own truth and dread,
its own ways of making people disappear.

I won't tell you where the place is, the dark mesh of the woods
meeting the unmarked strip of light—
ghost-ridden crossroads, leafmold paradise:
I know already who wants to buy it, sell it, make it disappear.

And I won't tell you where it is, so why do I tell you
anything? Because you still listen, because in times like these
to have you listen at all, it's necessary
to talk about trees.

1991

3

A New National Anthem

The truth is, I've never cared for the National
Anthem. If you think about it, it's not a good
song. Too high for most of us with "the rocket's
red glare" and then there are the bombs.
(Always, always, there is war and bombs.)
Once, I sang it at homecoming and threw
even the tenacious high school band off key.
But the song didn't mean anything, just a call
to the field, something to get through before
the pummeling of youth. And what of the stanzas
we never sing, the third that mentions "no refuge
could save the hireling and the slave"? Perhaps,
the truth is, every song of this country
has an unsung third stanza, something brutal
snaking underneath us as we blindly sing
the high notes with a beer sloshing in the stands
hoping our team wins. Don't get me wrong, I do
like the flag, how it undulates in the wind
like water, elemental, and best when it's humbled,
brought to its knees, clung to by someone who
has lost everything, when it's not a weapon,
when it flickers, when it folds up so perfectly
you can keep it until it's needed, until you can
love it again, until the song in your mouth feels
like sustenance, a song where the notes are sung
by even the ageless woods, the short-grass plains,
the Red River Gorge, the fistful of land left
unpoisoned, that song that's our birthright,
that's sung in silence when it's too hard to go on,
that sounds like someone's rough fingers weaving
into another's, that sounds like a match being lit
in an endless cave, the song that says my bones
are your bones, and your bones are my bones,
and isn't that enough?

Short Anthem for the General Strike

after Helen Adam

The unborn are giving speeches
In their domino bastilles
The maybe spirits spread across the land
Vibrations of the vertical
Make the horned owl climb
The robots of the violent are at hand
Diebold springs the latch
Of the merciless vault
Quartz crystals make parabolas below
Stars come out like dandruff
On the Senator's coat
As she throws her weight
In Wall Street's private boat

(chorus) There's a fire in water
          There's a noose of comfort
          There's an arc of comfort
          Don't drink oblivion

In sunken leather basements
Of a document exposed
Genet writes in a lexicon we dream
Gardeners sneak past gardens
When the fires are extra low
A source confirms the source in Pakistan
Now the shredder says woe-whoa
When grinding up the facts
Its Grendel-teeth work better in reverse
It will still be grinding
When the whole thing comes down
And a dolphin detour puts us back on course

(chorus) There's a fire in water
          There's a noose of comfort
          There's an arc of comfort
          Don't drink oblivion

What We Did in the Resistance (Part 1)

In the beginning, we wept.
Well, some of us wept.
Some of us walked around stunned
as if pieces of sky
had fallen out of the sky and revealed themselves
to be chunks of blue plaster.
We examined the chunks.
We shook plaster dust out of our hair—there was so much dust!
We craned our necks and stared up.
Now we saw the scaffolding,
the what-do-you-call-it—sheetrock?
The drywall, the lath. We saw the insulation,
full of asbestos, we saw how the walls were stuffed
with it, like money. Everything
was revealed, yet nothing was clear.
If we were in a cunningly devised structure
not of our making, was it a theater
or a prison, a shopping mall or a mausoleum?
In the beginning, as I have said, we wept.
And raged and questioned. We embraced on the street
when we saw each other. We sat together
in cafes drinking coffee, digesting our grief.
The rest of the time we sat in front of glowing screens.
We gathered at night and made signs:
Not My President and Pussy Grabs Back;
we stapled them to sticks
and marched in exultation all over the world.
We had never seen before how many of us there are.
We clicked and liked and signed and donated and called
our Congresspeople, and sent postcards and checks.
We spoke of girding ourselves for the long fight.
We spoke of a marathon, we spoke of walking
in the footsteps of the elders, we spoke
of coal miners in Pennsylvania and Kentucky

who had voted for Trump.
And still the cat box needed to be cleaned, the oil in the car changed,
classes taught, bills paid, dishes washed.
And still the rains came down, especially, biblically—
we joked about End Times—and the witching trees
with their bare black branches
sprouted the tiniest of new buds,
almost invisible at first, a red tip at the nodes, a subtle fire,
and then overnight, purple blossoms;
the trees who knew nothing of elections,
the trees who outweighed us and would outlast us
and despite everything the earth continued to turn
from light to darkness and into light again, over and over it rolled,
as it had been rolling through generations of empire and uprising,
extinction and evolution, and once again
to our surprise we noticed that it was spring.

SONNET XII: On the Detraction Which Followed Upon My Writing Certain Treatises

I did but prompt the age to quit their clogs
    By the known rules of ancient liberty,
    When straight a barbarous noise environs me
    Of owls and cuckoos, asses, apes and dogs;
As when those hinds that were transformed to frogs
    Railed at Latona's twin-born progeny
    Which after held the sun and moon in fee.
    But this is got by casting pearl to hogs
That bawl for freedom in their senseless mood
    And still revolt when truth would set them free—
    License they mean when they cry liberty;
For who loves that, must first be wise and good;
    But from that mark how far they rove we see,
    For all this waste of wealth and loss of blood.

Antigone Marches on Washington

When she casts herself as Antigone,
Audition for the part of Haemon.
She does not need another Creon in her life.
She does not need another blind follower of the figurehead blinded by hate.
She does not need another bigot to discredit the truth of prophets and the past.
She does not need another self-important king to tell her his rash laws outrank
  the laws of gods.
Men like that are the reason
She scatters the dust of revolution on those left to rot in the sun,
And will walk to the tomb for her cause.
Your mindless threats cannot sway her,
For she knows her actions are just,
That the king's are not based on morality,
So step out of her way,
For Athena's voice is her conscience,
And Hera's fury glows in her eyes,
And if you strike her, the goddesses above will see that you fall,
Will see that you realize your sin too late,
Will make you beg forgiveness in vain.

If you can see that Antigone marches in justice,
Go fill Haemon's shoes.
Warn that tyrant to think things through,
Tell him to listen to the people in the streets who whisper that he is wrong,
And if he will not listen,
Rise to fight with the maiden who follows her heart.
Be unafraid of what it takes to prove her voice is valid too,
For justice must come in the end, not from hands of gods, but from you.

What I know I cannot say

We sailed to Angel Island, and for several hours
I did not think of you. When I couldn't stop myself, finally,
from thinking of you, it was not really you but the trees,
not really the trees but their strange pods, blooming
for a while longer, a bloom more like the fringed fan
at the tip of a peacock's tail than anything I'd call a flower,
and so I was thinking about flowers and what we value
in a flower more than I was thinking of the island or its trees,
and much more than I was thinking of you. Recursive language
ties us together, linguists say. I am heading down this road.
I am heading down this road despite the caution signs
and the narrow shoulders. I am heading down the curvy road
despite the caution signs and the narrow shoulders
because someone I fell in love with once lived somewhere near. Right there,
that is an example of recursive language. Every language,
nearly every language, in the world demands recursion.
Few things bring us together more than our need to spell out
our intentions, which helps explain the early 20th-century
Chinese prisoners who scratched poems into walls on Angel Island,
and why a Polish detainee wrote his mother's name in 1922. I was here,
they wanted to tell us, and by here they meant the island
and they also meant the world. And by the island, they meant
the world they knew, and they also meant the world they left
and the world they wanted to believe could be theirs, the world they knew
required passwords. Think of the Angel Island Immigration Station as purgatory,
the guide explained. He told tales of paper fathers, picture brides,
the fabrications of familiarity so many lives depended on. Inquiries
demanded consistency despite the complications of interpretation.
In English one would ask: How many windows were in your house
in the village? How many ducks did you keep? What is the shape
of the birthmark on your father's left cheek? In Japanese, Cantonese,
Danish, Punjabi, the other answered. Then it all had to come back
to English. The ocean is wide and treacherous between one
home and the other. There can be no turning back, no correction
once what is said is said. Who can blame the Chinese detainees

who carved poems deep into the wood on Angel Island's walls.
Who can blame the Salvadoran who etched his village's name.
Few things tie us together more than our need to dig up the right words
to justify ourselves. Travelers and students, we sailed into the bay,
disembarked on Angel Island. I didn't think about you.
Which is to say, the blue gum eucalyptus is considered a threat,
though we brought it across oceans to help us. Desired first for its timber
because it grows quickly and so was expected to provide a practical fortune,
and when it did not, enlisted as a windbreak, desired still
because it is fast growing and practical, the blue gum has colonized
the California coastal forests, squeezing out native plants, dominating
the landscape, and increasing the danger of fire. I should hate
the blue gum eucalyptus, but from the well of their longing,
by which I mean to say from their pods, you know what I mean
I hope, their original homes, from the well of their longing
blooms explode like fireworks. I love them for this. Do you hear me?
I absolve you. You are far too beautiful and singular to blame.

Spirit Level

                                 A new country is formed
on the banks of the old, and its stories are still seedlings. Its citizens wait
for their private miracles to come

to pass. The new parliament hustles its alchemists back from breaking
rocks on the road and sets them to work.

Meanwhile everyone runs a little moonshine business
on the side.   Everyone pilots their narrow pirogue

back across the river of the old country and waves at their neighbors
from the opposite shore.
                                 How dim the light over there,
they think. How mud-colored the chickens. The threadbare river

runs thick with its tapestry of algae
                    fit only for snakes. The parliament spends days

sucking on the devil's nipple, their hair white as the ash
            of burned dockets, as the sun-bleached and sun-pocked bones

of a horse. Émigré punks take dust baths in the alleys. A man
who's sold sea sponges all his life boards up his windows. The scarlet ibis

he keeps in a cage and speaks with all day from his desk
                        dies abruptly of sorrow. The elderly,

who haven't taken leave of certainty since their time converting unbelievers
long ago, gather on the cathedral steps to brandish placards

at the face of heaven.   The young are burning up
their identity cards, stirring small fires set on the sidewalk

with sticks. The trees are golden with canaries still, a spirit level
for the foothills of revolution. It is as if the miraculous has suddenly—

my soon-to-be written protest poem

proves elusive and reluctant to speak but agrees to man up
    and join marchers

flies cross town to enter hotbed plaza where speakers, aggressive and sure,
    put silence to shame

retreats to slate-topped wall to curse being made of words where actions
    are needed

seeks memory of Bastille stones, Brandywine muskets, Selma blood,
    Kent State bullets

knows where right abides: here. demands of self: find courage and voice

swears to shout out its oneness with all who resist

considers a form: free, blank, haiku, villanelle? tone: fiery, cool, reflective, all?

decides that straightforward narrative with single lines
and occasional couplets (one rhymed) would be best

embraces these, feeling along its spine the payoff of standing tall
and the blood-connection of each and all

will put life on the line against fascism and all its kin

Where the Deer Find Refuge

I turn my back as winter sun sets
and a fat sparrow hops between leaves—
the full and the fallen.

I fix a cup of tea, milky and sweet
and worry a knot behind my shoulder blade—
my infallible corporal rosary.

There used to be a chapel in a building that no longer exists.

I mend my Bosnian slippers
and watch a boat go down the Ulanga River, 1914—
ripples and butterflies, ripples and butterflies.

There will be more time yet to cry, to rage, to hold each other.

I raise my pen to meet thick paper
and a crow struggles against the storm—
the necessary can feel futile.

There is a crack in the wood where the ants come in.

I welcome the jazz of rain on roof
and wonder where the deer find refuge.
Be grateful, be alert—hard rains, hard rains.

Ode

He who ordered the death
of six thousand kept
Goethe at his bedside
and loved Brahms beyond measure.

He who poisoned his brother
wept before a painting
of the Virgin and Child
and gladly would have killed to possess it.

Are there two worlds, one
of Sabbath beauty, the other,
well, the "harsh reality,"
a prison house for all alike?

Is this Achilles' shield,
the arts of peace covering
the shame of naked force,
a layer of lies and then the truth?

Temples of holy spirit,
caves of demons, cells
of reason and bad dreams,
we humans have many arts.

And they're not always offered
with clean hands. Would you,
Herr Wagner, be so kind
as to rise and show us your hands? *Danke.*

Better perhaps the art
we love be not too much
better than we, lest it
excuse us from being any better.

Best, I think, to pray
for a conscience that spares nothing,
not art, not us, not love.
That is the highest art, that love.

Love in a Year of Outrage

When you shouted *there it is!*—
like a spiritual awakening—
I ran to see, expecting
I don't know what, maybe
the wedding ring you lost our first year,
an alien ship, or some extinct beast
big-footing it up the drive.
It was dusk and cold and the most
hyperbolic of times. This land
that called out to my ancestors felt so foreign
I thought I should dig up my dead and move.
It was the end of a day, but felt
like the End of Days. You stood
at the French doors facing the dunes
and peering through binoculars, eager
for me to look up from my dread
and see whatever it was you saw.
In a notch about two inches above the horizon
and sinking fast, the planet Mercury—
a small, golden point
I never would have noticed without you.
The planets continue to hold,
three of them visible last night: Mercury
aglow, reddish Mars, and Venus constant
in our evenings. We are changed.
Yet we're not. I don't know another way
to say it better than how Mercury says it,
remaining where it should, predictable
in the best of ways, exuding the warm color of gold
worn on the hand for a long time, a pinprick ablaze
for longer than our species will exist,
living its only life as light. Between us
and it, there's a distance far beyond air,
and beyond despair.

Hard Winter

Mourning What We Thought We Were

We were born into an amazing experiment.

At least we thought we were. We knew there was no
escaping human nature: my grandmother

taught me that: my own pitiless nature
taught me that: but we exist inside an order, I

thought, of which history
is the mere shadow—

*

Every serious work of art about America has the same
theme: *America*

is a great Idea: the reality leaves something to be desired.

Bakersfield. Marian Anderson, first great black classical
contralto, whom the Daughters of the American Revolution

would not allow to sing in an unsegregated

Constitution Hall, who then was asked by Eleanor
Roosevelt to sing at the Lincoln Memorial before thousands

was refused a room at the Padre Hotel, Bakersfield.

My mother's disgust
as she told me this. It confirmed her judgment about

what she never could escape, where she lived out her life.

My grandmother's fury when, at the age of seven or
eight, I had eaten at the home of a black friend.

The forced camps at the end of *The Grapes of Wrath*
were outside

Bakersfield. When I was a kid, *Okie*

was still a common
term of casual derision and contempt.

*

So it was up to us, born
in Bakersfield, to carve a new history

of which history is the mere shadow—

*

To further the history of the spirit is our work:

therefore thank you, Lord
Whose Bounty Proceeds by Paradox,

for showing us we have failed to change.

*

Dark night, December 1st 2016.

White supremacists, once again in
America, are acceptable, respectable. America!

Bakersfield was first swamp, then
desert. We are sons of the desert
who cultivate the top half-inch of soil.

I imagined all the place names as code

As a way of approaching a river; a kind of gill net.
Willamette and Chehalis; verso and recto.

As aperture. As moon in Libra. Absolute somehow.
As one who says simply, *you ask me and thus.*

I think I imagined a kind of beak. I think I imagined
a list of long-ish words. As one might philosophize

about the thaw while pumping gas;
the way one might pump gas, staring blankly

at the small red blizzard of numbers,
seeing a school of fish.

I have always imagined Paradise
as doing many things in a small space.

Oh, tarp. Oh, evergreens in snow—
there is no one to tell this story to.

A Poetry Reading at West Point

I read to the entire plebe class,
in two batches. Twice the hall filled
with bodies dressed alike, each toting
a copy of my book. What would my
shrink say, if I had one, about
such a dream, if it were a dream?

Question and answer time.
"Sir," a cadet yelled from the balcony,
and gave his name and rank, and then,
closing his parentheses, yelled
"Sir" again. "Why do your poems give
me a headache when I try

to understand them?" he asked.
"Do you want that?" I have a gift for
gentle jokes to defuse tension,
but this was not the time to use it.
"I try to write as well as I can
what it feels like to be human,"

I started, picking my way care-
fully, for he and I were, after
all, pained by the same dumb longings.
"I try to say what I don't know
how to say, but of course I can't
get much of it down at all."

By now I was sweating bullets.
"I don't want my poems to be hard,
unless the truth is, if there is
a truth." Silence hung in the hall
like a heavy fabric. My own
head ached. "Sir," he yelled. "Thank you. Sir."

Perhaps

Reply to the Loneliness of a Poet

Perhaps our hearts
    will have no reader
Perhaps we took the wrong road
    and so we end up lost

Perhaps we light one lantern after another
    storms blow them out one by one
Perhaps we burn our life candle against the dark
    but no fire warms the body

Perhaps once we're out of tears
    the land will be fertilized
Perhaps while we praise the sun
    we are also sung by the sun

Perhaps the heavier the monkey on our shoulders
    the more we believe
Perhaps we can only protest others' suffering
    silent to our own misfortune
Perhaps
    because this call is irresistible
        we have no other choice

Translated by Tony Barnstone and Newton Liu

Gate A-4

Wandering around the Albuquerque Airport Terminal, after learning my flight had been delayed four hours, I heard an announcement: "If anyone in the vicinity of Gate A-4 understands any Arabic, please come to the gate immediately."

Well—one pauses these days. Gate A-4 was my own gate. I went there.

An older woman in full traditional Palestinian embroidered dress, just like my grandma wore, was crumpled to the floor, wailing. "Help," said the flight agent. "Talk to her. What is her problem? We told her the flight was going to be late and she did this."

I stooped to put my arm around the woman and spoke haltingly. "Shu-dow-a, Shu-bid-uck Hahbibti? Stani schway, Min fadlick, Shu-bit se-wee?" The minute she heard any words she knew, however poorly used, she stopped crying. She thought the flight had been cancelled entirely. She needed to be in El Paso for major medical treatment the next day. I said, "No, we're fine, you'll get there, just later, who is picking you up? Let's call him."

We called her son, I spoke with him in English. I told him I would stay with his mother till we got on the plane and ride next to her. She talked to him. Then we called her other sons just for the fun of it. Then we called my dad and he and she spoke for a while in Arabic and found out of course they had ten shared friends. Then I thought just for the heck of it why not call some Palestinian poets I know and let them chat with her? This all took up two hours.

She was laughing a lot by then. Telling of her life, patting my knee, answering questions. She had pulled a sack of homemade *mamool* cookies—little powdered sugar crumbly mounds stuffed with dates and nuts—from her bag—and was offering them to all the women at the gate. To my amazement, not a single woman declined one. It was like a sacrament. The traveler from Argentina, the mom from California, the lovely woman from Laredo—we were all covered with the same powdered sugar. And smiling. There is no better cookie.

And then the airline broke out free apple juice from huge coolers and two
little girls from our flight ran around serving it and they
were covered with powdered sugar, too. And I noticed my new best friend—
by now we were holding hands—had a potted plant poking out of her bag,
some medicinal thing, with green furry leaves. Such an old-country
tradition. Always carry a plant. Always stay rooted to somewhere.

And I looked around that gate of late and weary ones and I thought, This
is the world I want to live in. The shared world. Not a single person in that
gate—once the crying of confusion stopped—seemed apprehensive about
any other person. They took the cookies. I wanted to hug all those other
women, too.

This can still happen anywhere. Not everything is lost.

Hard Winter

for Naomi

Everywhere I go, people are shouting
at one another, people are shaking

their fists at one another. Everywhere
I go, I see someone knapping

an edge to a stone. I want to begin
to carry a plant from another epoch,

perhaps the Pleistocene, wherever I travel.
I'll have my friend, who is a potter, shape

the iridium clay from a previous extinction
into a vessel that fits the roots

and the palm of my hand. Everywhere
I go, the plant I carry will always be

in blossom, its fragrance sweet, but not
like those rainforest plants that mimic

rotten flesh. The flower of the plant I carry
will smell like a cheap white dress shirt

fresh off the line. The petals will be as fragile
as a man, thin as a photograph and forever

standing before dirty tanks in an otherwise
empty square. I will be surrounded

by honeybees, jostling pistils and stamens
until the dust falls, like powdered sugar,

onto our knuckles and knees, onto our animal
bodies, soft as a tongue. The vibration

of uncountable wings in motion all around me
will cast out the treaded sounds of war.

Alternative Facts

I'm worried about truth, that it's a hunger, that we've already eaten too much and are too full to know when to stop. (a heavy drinker vs. an alcoholic) (flood gate vs. rain fall) (non-non-non-fiction) (read: it's messy) (read: we must try) (read: colonial power involves putting people into categories) (check the box) (sign an oath of allegiance) (American, red blood, blue blood—this depends on the air and if the blood has left my body) (I should have finished this poem before the election) (now I am mourning and fatalistic and knitting a pink hat) tyranny does not begin in violence, it begins with the first act of collaboration. slap my hand over the tight orange leather ball. game on. I was wondering what I would do with my life. now I see I will be filling sandbags for rising water. I will be trying to reach Dianne Feinstein on the phone. I will make myself a place of safe harbor. DACA students, people without papers, people who carry scientific knowledge, people who pray. I will start before they come for me. I have no tattoos. I have not spent a night in jail. I have two passports, three bank accounts, my name on a marriage license, a house deed, dental records, blood type, insurance card, driver's license. I will be hard to erase. but not impossible.

Why We Believe Obvious Untruths

My father once filmed a stop-action scene
of presents filling up under the tree, proof

that Santa Claus was invisible but real.
I stuck to my guns before I was given guns,

even before I became a teenage interrogator,
learning Russian from defectors, practicing

techniques to find the weak point in others
and exploit how the truth was malleable.

Our loved ones begin the parade with obvious
half-lies on how we look or that everything

will be fine when we don't know if the future
holds mud pie or devil's food cake. We are told we

will be able to lift ourselves by our bootstraps,
one of the reasons why my parents kicked me

out and I joined the Army, too young to know
that belief is the paralyzing absence of fear,

dangerous in the way waving your hand over
a flame might change the annals of history.

Ideas are news. Ideas are insane. Ideas are art.
Inside us, inside the earth. Whistles in the dark.

We sprinkle secret desires into tales whipped
into batter, baked, and served to oohs and aahs,

taste the concoctions that make us purse our lips
from a disastrous recipe now mistaken for a kiss.

An Iris for Hillary, January 20, 2017: A Cento

My Portion is Defeat—today—
Dark incandescent winds blow.

The test begins.
In the terminal of stopped time I went unsteady to the beat.

Having given up hope for a high-wire act,

my mother has been singing ghazals in the crypt,
no strings, no mirrors, no

stasis in darkness.
Someday we will take this chance again.

An iris understands intake and wait,
sugar shimmering in the veins.

Emily Dickinson, No. 639 ("My Portion Is Defeat"); Audre Lorde, "Starting All Over Again"; Kay Ryan, "Rats' Tails"; Joy Harjo, "Everybody Has a Heartache: A Blues"; Colleen J. McElroy, "Learning to Swim at Forty-Five"; Bhanu Kapil, "What Are the Consequences of Silence"; Maxine Hong Kingston, "I Love a Broad Margin to My Life"; Sylvia Plath, "Ariel"; Joan Swift, "Poem"; Malinda Markham, "Body from Scratch"; Ruth Thompson, "Spring Along Cazenovia Creek"

The great tablecloth

When they were called to the table,
the tyrants came rushing
with their temporary ladies;
it was fine to watch the women pass
like wasps with big bosoms
followed by those pale
and unfortunate public tigers.

The peasant in the field ate
his poor quota of bread,
he was alone, it was late,
he was surrounded by wheat,
but he had no more bread;
he ate it with grim teeth,
looking at it with hard eyes.

In the blue hour of eating,
the infinite hour of the roast,
the poet abandons his lyre,
takes up his knife and fork,
puts his glass on the table,
and the fishermen attend
the little sea of the soup bowl.
Burning potatoes protest
among the tongues of oil.
The lamb is gold on its coals
and the onion undresses.
It is sad to eat in dinner clothes,
like eating in a coffin,
but eating in convents
is like eating underground.
Eating alone is a disappointment,
but not eating matters more,
is hollow and green, has thorns
like a chain of fish hooks
trailing from the heart,
clawing at your insides.

Hunger feels like pincers,
like the bite of crabs,
it burns, burns and has no fire.
Hunger is a cold fire.
Let us sit down soon to eat
with all those who haven't eaten;
let us spread great tablecloths,
put salt in the lakes of the world,
set up planetary bakeries,
tables with strawberries in snow,
and a plate like the moon itself
from which we can all eat.

For now I ask no more
than the justice of eating.

Translated by Alastair Reid

From the Republic of Conscience

I

When I landed in the republic of conscience
it was so noiseless when the engines stopped
I could hear a curlew high above the runway.

At immigration, the clerk was an old man
who produced a wallet from his homespun coat
and showed me a photograph of my grandfather.

The woman in customs asked me to declare
the words of our traditional cures and charms
to heal dumbness and avert the evil eye.

No porters. No interpreter. No taxi.
You carried your own burden and very soon
your symptoms of creeping privilege disappeared.

II

Fog is a dreaded omen there but lightning
spells universal good and parents hang
swaddled infants in trees during thunderstorms.

Salt is their precious mineral. And seashells
are held to the ear during births and funerals.
The base of all inks and pigments is seawater.

Their sacred symbol is a stylized boat.
The sail is an ear, the mast a sloping pen,
the hull a mouth-shape, the keel an open eye.

At their inauguration, public leaders
must swear to uphold unwritten law and weep
to atone for their presumption to hold office—

and to affirm their faith that all life sprang
from salt in tears which the sky-god wept
after he dreamt his solitude was endless.

III

I came back from that frugal republic
with my two arms the one length, the customs
woman having insisted my allowance was myself.

The old man rose and gazed into my face
and said that was official recognition
that I was now a dual citizen.

He therefore desired me when I got home
to consider myself a representative
and to speak on their behalf in my own tongue.

Their embassies, he said, were everywhere
but operated independently
and no ambassador would ever be relieved.

A Phoenix Flag

In the basin, the sun sears fabric
to its barest fiber, while the snap and rustle
of daily activity frays edges, rusts eyelets.

Desert air hangs still. The flag wilts,
paled now to the fragile pink, gray,
and blue of a heat-burnt sky.

No matter the age and tearing,
the momentum of a moment's breeze
never ceases to call the flag to rise.

Ragged, the banner yet braves,
whips, cracks against the wind,
hung long ago by a sporadic patriot.

For yes, yes, it always answers,
its fading colors flourishing endurance,
its tattered clothes climbing high

to show itself upon the cloudless sky
as a journey without destination,
as a repeated rise from collapse.

The End and the Beginning

War Voyeurs

for Clara Fraser

I do not understand why men make war.

Is it because artillery is the most stoic example
of what flesh can become?
Is it because the military plan is the final map
drawn by the wisest hunter?
Is it because the neutron ray is the invincible finger
no one will disobey?

or

Is it because the flood of blood is the proper penance
workers must pay for failing tribute at the prescribed
hour?

I do not understand why men make war.

Is it because when death is multiple and expanding, there
among the odd assemblages, arbitrary and unnamed, there
among the shriveled mountains, distorted and hollow, there
among the liquid farms and cities, cold and sallow, there
among the splintered bones of children, women, men, and cattle,
there and only there, the eerie head of power is being born?

Is it because submission is the only gesture to be rehearsed,
to be dressed, to be modeled, to be cast, to be chosen
in the one and only one drama to be staged in the theater of
this world, where everyone must act with the backbone humbled
with the mascara of bondage, with the lipstick of slaves under
the light of gentle assassination with applause piercing the ground
forever?

or

Is it because war is the secret room of all things to be kept
sealed and contained, to be conquered and renamed *woman,*
enclosed by an empire of walls, vaults, hinges, and locks with
the hot key that men and only men must possess for an eternal
evening to visit and contemplate, to snap open a favorite window
and gaze at the calibrated murder as lovers of beauty?

The Ones Without Names

saw grunts cut off Charlie's ear to confirm a kill
saw these lugholes stowed in gunny sacks saw some guys
in Tiger Force recon wear them as necklaces or medals
saw them take not one but both ears to boot up the count
heard COs savvy to this ruse divide that number by two
then order GIs to cut and scoop the anus out instead
saw piles of man holes dried to hardtack treasured as trophies
saw hootches and huts burned down as M16s played taps
saw grenades launched into batches of women and children
read in *Stars & Stripes* how hawks on the home front growled
and hooted and groused about honor about dying to try out
new toxic agents and bigger bombs saw snapshots of doves
cooing for peace booing against war and peaceniks marching
for a pullout and the brass in the Pentagon bottleneck
goose-stepping and crowing in headlines and subheads
about light at the end of their tunnel
about the prey in a gunsight

Song

Oh God, she said

It began a beautiful day by the sunup.
And we sat in our grove of trees and smiles
Morning eggs and toast and jam
Long talks and baby babble
Becky sitting in her chair
Spreading goo in her hair.

Oh God, she said, look at the baby

Saying *hi, ho, ha, hi hi, goggydoggymammadada HI*
And the light was coming through the window
Through the handprints on the glass
Making shadow patterns, and the cold day
Was bright outside and they were muddling
In their underwear, getting dressed
Putting diapers on the baby, slipping
Sandals on her feet.

Oh God, she said, look at the baby
He has blood all over him, she cried

Then the postman came
And she went out on the steps
To get her magazine. And they stood
By the stairs and looked, the baby
Tugging at her skirt saying
Mamammama upupup mememe
As she looked at the pictures of Song My.

Oh God, she said, look at the baby
He has blood all over, she cried
Look at that woman's face, my God,
She knows she's going to get it.

Going to get it, they knew
They were going to get it
And it was a beautiful day
The day that began in the fields
With the golden grain against the sky
The babies singing as if there were not
Soldiers in the air.

1969

Aubade with Burning City

South Vietnam, April 29, 1975: Armed Forces Radio played Irving Berlin's "White Christmas" as a code to begin Operation Frequent Wind, the ultimate evacuation of American civilians and Vietnamese refugees by helicopter during the fall of Saigon.

Milkflower petals on the street
                      like pieces of a girl's dress.

May your days be merry and bright . . .

He fills a teacup with champagne, brings it to her lips.
     Open, he says.
             She opens.
                      Outside, a soldier spits out
       his cigarette as footsteps fill the square like stones
                       fallen from the sky. *May*
all your Christmases be white
           as the traffic guard unstraps his holster.

         His fingers running the hem
of her white dress. A single candle.
         Their shadows: two wicks.

A military truck speeds through the intersection, the sound of children
               shrieking inside. A bicycle hurled
   through a store window. When the dust rises, a black dog
        lies panting in the road. Its hind legs
                    crushed into the shine
              8of a white Christmas.

On the bed stand, a sprig of magnolia expands like a secret heard
                    for the first time.

The treetops glisten and children listen, the chief of police
        facedown in a pool of Coca-Cola.
           A palm-sized photo of his father soaking
   beside his left ear.

The song moving through the city like a widow.
      A white . . . A white . . . I'm dreaming of a curtain of snow

                falling from her shoulders.

Snow scraping against the window. Snow shredded
            with gunfire. Red sky.
         Snow on the tanks rolling over the city walls.
A helicopter lifting the living just
                       out of reach.

      The city so white it is ready for ink.

           The radio saying run run run.
Milkflower petals on a black dog
        like pieces of a girl's dress.

May your days be merry and bright. She is saying
       something neither of them can hear. The hotel rocks
         beneath them. The bed a field of ice.

Don't worry, he says, as the first shell flashes
         their faces, *my brothers have won the war*
              and tomorrow . . .
        The lights go out.

I'm dreaming. I'm dreaming . . .
               to hear sleigh bells in the snow . . .

In the square below: a nun, on fire,
           runs silently toward her god—

      Open, he says.
             She opens.

Thanks

Thanks for the tree
between me & a sniper's bullet.
I don't know what made the grass
sway seconds before the Viet Cong
raised his soundless rifle.
Some voice always followed,
telling me which foot
to put down first.
Thanks for deflecting the ricochet
against that anarchy of dusk.
I was back in San Francisco
wrapped up in a woman's wild colors,
causing some dark bird's love call
to be shattered by daylight
when my hands reached up
& pulled a branch away
from my face. Thanks
for the vague white flower
that pointed to the gleaming metal
reflecting how it is to be broken
like mist over the grass,
as we played some deadly
game for blind gods.
What made me spot the monarch
writhing on a single thread
tied to a farmer's gate,
holding the day together
like an unfingered guitar string,
is beyond me. Maybe the hills
grew weary & leaned a little in the heat.
Again, thanks for the dud
hand grenade tossed at my feet
outside Chu Lai. I'm still
falling through its silence.

I don't know why the intrepid
sun touched the bayonet,
but I know that something
stood among those lost trees
& moved only when I moved.

Mother, Flying

In the front hallway
two men
standing tall
in blue uniforms;
one removes his cap,
the other stares
without blinking.
Before they can speak,
she feels herself disappear.

*

The next night in a dream
she's flying low
across the Afghan desert,
passing over
her son's white crib in the sand,
the ladder to his tree house.
"Hey," she calls out,
"hey."

Rabbit

a mother and the son
      who went to war
talked of the poetry she wrote
describing how he changed
      about the things
      that changed him

he'd never hunted
      so her son was picked
      in a survival test
to be the first in his platoon
      to kill a rabbit
his sergeant told him
      how to rock the creature in his arms
      gently at first
      then harder
until it stopped struggling
      lay calm
      and cuddled motionless against him
that was the cue to smash its head
      against a tree
he said it squeaked a bit
      just a few squeaks before it died

the poems formed a bridge
      between the two
they helped me know her better
      said the son
the mother said they helped her understand
      what he'd become

Black Powder

In the beginning the powder was without
the form of the gun to hold it.

The Alchemist said
Let there be explosions of bamboo,
wicks burning incendiary dust to ignition.
And the shrapnel of centuries swarmed across the world.

And He said
Let them shrink the barrel to the size of an arm
on fire, glory at the form glory takes:
blood's warm liquidity
surging from bird and beast.
And the Alchemist made the adrenaline
of the pulled trigger.

And the Alchemist said
The mountains are too much.
Let us separate the earth from its interior.
And so they bestowed arteries upon the expanse,
serpentine hollows to carry the railways
that carried Men through their dominion.

And the Men exploded the railways
in His image. And the Men opened fire
in crowded theatres, in elementary schools.
And the Women fired at wolves
from the safety of a helicopter.
And the Soldiers fired on the Soldiers
and the Men and the Women, on the Children,
and they set fire to the fields, and every new invention
was a synapse firing through the brain, bearing
new ways to fire: nitroglycerin, nitrocellulose,
trinitrotoluene, dynamite, C-4, pressurized gas.
And the synapses bore the fissile isotopes:
uranium-235, plutonium-239.

And the Alchemist said unto them all
Be fruitful, multiply your arms, your weapons caches
so you may assure our mutual destruction
and that of all which moves upon the earth.
And the Men and the Women
were fruitful. Behold.

Z.

Zone of fire[1]—An area into which a designated ground unit or fire support
ship delivers, or is prepared to deliver, fire support. Fire may or may not be
observed. Also called ZF. (JP3-O9)

The alphabet keepers have delivered. In numerical order.
Children + you + us + hordes of them across the sea are
designated to an area of our nation's soundproofed cells
rocking back and forth with our soldiers home again gone
home gone again home again and still coming home while you
keep looking in the lost and found for limbs and reasons.

In war rooms cooks are serving bits and pieces of tidbits
to generals balanced on a beam tip supporting an industry
driven by bearded cab drivers whose minds are filled with
maps of other homelands stuck in rush hour on their way to
window displays lined with row upon row of splendid shoes
flashing on the feet of athletes soaring towards the net
their skin parchments of poems and bankers losing count
of moaning parents + brothers + sisters = all the aching.

Speeches are slipping on sheets of conscripted words
lulling us to sleep > our dreams mutilated and chained
in cellars of popped lullabies and million dollar prizes
stopped at a stop sign of broken tail lights surrounded by
weeping relatives marching and we are marching + marching
towards that written-off place we glimpsed in childhood.

Love. Whatever. Toss with Roundup® and serve for dinner.
Waters are rising. Who cares when you can barely recall
what truth tastes like on the tip of your outstretched tongue.
The sky is falling from behind the stars nailed to the flag.
Spin all these words and tumble dry on high. Send a postcard.
Write: XXXXXXXXXXXXXXXXXXXXXXXX. Observe your fire and support.
Remember I love you and that the alphabet is free. Take it.
Eat the letters[E] [M] [P] [I] [R][E]. Then form a new word outside
the zone of fire. You may or may not be observed +/- followed.

---

[1]*Second-to-last entry in the United States Department of Defense's* Dictionary of Military
and Associated Terms, *October 17, 2007*

Winged and Acid Dark

A sentence with "dappled shadow" in it.
Something not sayable
spurting from the morning silence,
secret as a thrush.

The other man, the officer, who brought onions
and wine and sacks of flour,
the major with the swollen knee,
wanted intelligent conversation afterward.
Having no choice, she provided that, too.

Potsdamerplatz, May 1945.

When the first one was through he pried her mouth open.
Bashō told Rensetsu to avoid sensational materials.
If the horror of the world were the truth of the world,
he said, there would be no one to say it
and no one to say it to.
I think he recommended describing the slightly frenzied
swarming of insects near a waterfall.

Pried her mouth open and spit in it.
We pass these things on,
probably, because we are what we can imagine.

Something not sayable in the morning silence.
The mind hungering after likenesses. "Tender sky," etc.,
curves the swallows trace in air.

Why I Don't Mention Flowers
When Conversations with My Brother
Reach Uncomfortable Silences

*Forgive me, distant wars, for bringing
flowers home.*
—WISŁAWA SZYMBORSKA

In the Kashmir mountains,
my brother shot many men,
blew skulls from brown skins,
dyed white desert sand crimson.

What is there to say to a man
who has traversed such a world,
whose hands and eyes have
betrayed him?

Were there flowers there? I asked.

This is what he told me:

In a village, many men
wrapped a woman in a sheet.
She didn't struggle.
Her bare feet dragged in the dirt.

They laid her in the road
and stoned her.

The first man was her father.
He threw two stones in a row.
Her brother had filled his pockets
with stones on the way there.

The crowd was a hive
of disturbed bees. The volley
of stones against her body
drowned out her moans.

Blood burst through the sheet
like a patch of violets,
a hundred roses in bloom.

American Dream with Exit Wound

She looks at the belts differently now
Not at the grain, the tool work

Not thinking what size for which waist
She looks at where the holes are

One punched out with a nail file
a peeler, dug out with a stick

blunt but strong enough
to grind out a hole in leather

A hole too close to the buckle

She looks at his belts for a hole
too close to the buckle

Belt, tourniquet, cinch—
The cubital vein pops up

blue as a bruise
a swollen lip

The sting is brief
endurable

And all that is unendurable
melts into air

Hectoring voices
stilled

Enemies pierced
through

Achilles at last asleep in his tent
His pillow wet

The warm blue Aegean
slipping over it

Letter to My Country in Wartime

All I hear in the U.S. is U.
I used to love U.
Shaped like a cup to be filled
To the brim by
Your people, your children,
All free to be strong, wrong
And in between,
All free to sing
On and off key
The very sound of U. flexing
Your lips
To a kiss . . .
But the U. that is You
These days
Is Ugly, Unsmiling, is most of the uns
That undo our heroes
And usher in outlaws.
U. go to war.
U. bomb and kill
U. want to rule
U. want to fill
The world with your
Uniform, uninformed, opus of order.
How can I be with U. anymore?
How can I take the Me out of U.?
What can I do? Go sit in the corner?
Refuse to play? Refuse to pay?
Get out of the car? Phone a lawyer?
File for divorce? Get on my horse
And ride away? Ride where?
You, U., are everywhere.
And nothing I
Can say or do
Will stop U. from
Taking all of US
Under.

The End and the Beginning

After every war
someone has to clean up.
Things won't
straighten themselves up, after all.

Someone has to push the rubble
to the side of the road,
so the corpse-filled wagons
can pass.

Someone has to get mired
in scum and ashes,
sofa springs,
splintered glass,
and bloody rags.

Someone has to drag in a girder
to prop up a wall.
Someone has to glaze a window,
rehang a door.

Photogenic it's not,
and takes years.
All the cameras have left
for another war.

We'll need the bridges back,
and new railway stations.
Sleeves will go ragged
from rolling them up.

Someone, broom in hand,
still recalls the way it was.
Someone else listens

and nods with unsevered head.
But already there are those nearby
starting to mill about
who will find it dull.

From out of the bushes
sometimes someone still unearths
rusted-out arguments
and carries them to the garbage pile.

Those who knew
what was going on here
must make way for
those who know little.
And less than little.
And finally as little as nothing.

In the grass that has overgrown
causes and effects,
someone must be stretched out
blade of grass in his mouth
gazing at the clouds

Translated by Joanna Trzeciak

American Towns

Seneca, Missouri—soft wash of casino jangle
seeps through the Pontiac's cracked window.

The map flutters on the dashboard,
one corner grit-soaked.

Sparse Ozark wash of tawny green.
A herd of buffalo lowing in the side pasture.

Here is the voyage,
conjured homeland to conjured homeland.

No, not that clawed trajectory of the past,
but a fierce conception

that quickens and scrapes inside just the same.
The drive to Ohio will take

eleven hours and forty-eight minutes,
cost one hundred and ninety-five dollars in gas.

Chillicothe—in the subtle semantics
of Shawnee, a tightened fist of connotation:

clan name and principal city,
all human systems working in harmony.

Limpid sashay of corn tassels along the byway.
Historical markers beckon the reader

to plunge an arm into the loam
tweeze with fingers to feel how fecund,

no rocks to bend the ploughshare.
What heirloom fields of Shawnee

corn hum under the crust
beside the carbon of burned council houses?

August wheeze of Bad Axe Creek.
Drought thrusts large boulders jutting up waist-high,

deep grooves in the center
for grinding corn. What is owed

grits in the corners of the mouth.
The plaque on the museum's door in Xenia extols

a Revolutionary War hero:
The ground on which this council house stands is unstained

with blood and is pure as my heart which wishes
for nothing so much as peace and brotherly love.

Summer school kids mill around the museum.
The teacher introduces the panel of tribal council members

as *remnants of the once great Shawnee tribe.*
Listless murmur of pencils across paper.

In the front room, a volunteer curator leans over a diorama
anxious to capture the real story

of a Revolutionary War camp.
He stipples red paint onto the sandy ground

simulating the gore of a military flogging,
points with the paintbrush to the next room

where fifty-three letters from 1783 broker captive trades
with the Delaware and Shawnee:

wan shades of ink from blanched olive to cornflower,
blotted in the rough or refined sway of long dead hands

each one made phylum by the promise of whiskey.
Leaving Xenia that evening on an old Shawnee trade route

retraced in concrete: Monlutha's Town, Wapakoneta,
Blue Jacket's Town, Mackachack, Wapotomica.

Xenia—the influence of the pollen
upon the form of the fruit.

I want my ink to bellow—
where is this ground unstained with blood?

The Dancing

In all these rotten shops, in all this broken furniture
and wrinkled ties and baseball trophies and coffee pots
I have never seen a postwar Philco
with the automatic eye
nor heard Ravel's "Bolero" the way I did
in 1945 in that tiny living room
on Beechwood Boulevard, nor danced as I did
then, my knives all flashing, my hair all streaming,
my mother red with laughter, my father cupping
his left hand under his armpit, doing the dance
of old Ukraine, the sound of his skin half drum,
half fart, the world at last a meadow,
the three of us whirling and singing, the three of us
screaming and falling, as if we were dying,
as if we could never stop—in 1945—
in Pittsburgh, beautiful filthy Pittsburgh, home
of the evil Mellons, 5,000 miles away
from the other dancing—in Poland and Germany—
oh God of mercy, oh wild God.

Violaceae

If we must have violence, then let it be
the violence of violets, how they burst
into spring, before most anything else—
vanguard of the voluptuous—
unravelling their petals, their leaves
to attract whatever will love them.
If we must rant and rave, than let us
do so as they do, inconspicuously,
close to the ground, in all the wet places
until something with a stinger comes
and mounts us, turning us inward
where we learn what it is to sweeten.

Jubilee Blues

because white men can't
police their imagination
black men are dying

dear white america

i've left Earth in search of darker planets, a solar system revolving too near a black hole. i've left in search of a new God. i do not trust the God you have given us. my grandmother's hallelujah is only outdone by the fear she nurses every time the blood-fat summer swallows another child who used to sing in the choir. take your God back. though his songs are beautiful his miracles are inconsistent. i want the fate of Lazarus for Renisha, want Chucky, Bo, Meech, Trayvon, Sean & Jonylah risen three days after their entombing, their ghost re-gifted flesh & blood, their flesh & blood re-gifted their children. i've left Earth, I am equal parts sick of your *go back to Africa* & *i just don't see race.* neither did the poplar tree. we did not build your boats (though we did leave a trail of kin to guide us home). we did not build your prisons (though we did & we fill them too). we did not ask to be part of your America (though are we not America? her joints brittle & dragging a ripped gown through Oakland?). i can't stand your ground. i'm sick of calling your recklessness the law. each night, i count my brothers. & in the morning, when some do not survive to be counted, i count the holes they leave. i reach for black folks & touch only air. your master magic trick, America. now he's breathing, now he don't. abra-cadaver. white bread voodoo. sorcery you claim not to practice, hand my cousin a pistol to do your work. i tried, white people. i tried to love you, but you spent my brother's funeral making plans for brunch, talking too loud next to his bones. you took one look at the river, plump with the body of boy after girl after sweet boi & ask *why does it always have to be about race?* because you made it that way! because you put an asterisk on my sister's gorgeous face! call her pretty (for a black girl)! because black girls go missing without so much as a whisper of where?! because there are no amber alerts for amber-skinned girls! because Jordon boomed. because Emmett whistled. because Huey P. spoke. because Martin preached. because black boys can always be too loud to live. because it's taken my papa's & my grandma's time, my father's time, my mother's time, my aunt's time, my uncle's time, my brother's & my sister's time . . . how much time do you want for your progress? i've left Earth to find a place where my kin can be safe, where black people ain't but people the same color as the good, wet earth, until that means something, until then i bid you well, i bid you war, i bid you our lives to gamble with no more. i've left Earth & i am touching everything you beg your telescopes to show you. i'm giving the stars their right names. & this life, this new story & history you cannot steal or sell or cast overboard or hang or beat or drown or own or redline or shackle or silence or cheat or choke or cover up or jail or shoot or jail or shoot or jail or shoot or ruin

this, if only this one, is ours.

When I Think of Tamir Rice While Driving

in the backseat, my sons laugh & tussle,
far from Tamir's age, adorned with his
complexion & cadence, & already warned

about toy pistols, though my rhetoric
ain't about fear, but dislike—about
how guns have haunted me since I first gripped

a pistol; I think of Tamir, blink away a tear
& confront weeping's inadequacy, how
some loss invents the geometry that baffles.

The Second Amendment—cold, cruel,
a constitutional violence, a ruthless
thing worrying me, should be it predicts

the heft in my hand, arm sag, burdened by,
with what I bear. My bare arms collaged
with wings as if hope alone can bring

back a buried child. A child, a toy gun,
a blue shield's rapid rapid rabid shit. This
is how misery sounds: my boys

playing in the backseat juxtaposed against
a twelve-year-old's murder playing
in my head. My tongue clings to the roof

of my mouth; my right hand has forgotten.
This is the brick & mortar of the America
that murdered Tamir & may stalk the laughter

in my backseat. I am a father driving
his black sons to school & the death
of a black boy rides shotgun as if this

could be a funeral procession, the death
a silent thing in the air unmentioned,
because mentioning death invites taboo:

if you touch my sons the blood washed
away from the concrete must, at some
point, belong to you, & not just to you, to

the artifice of justice that is draped like a blue
god around your shoulders, the badge that
justifies the echo of the fired pistol; taboo:

the thing that says freedom is a murder's body
mangled and disrupted by my constitutional
rights come to bear because the killer's mind

refused the narrative of a brown child, his dignity,
his right to breathe, his actual fucking existence
with all the crystalline brilliance I saw when

my boys first reached for me; this world best
invite more than story of the children bleeding
on crisp fall days, Tamir's death must be more

than warning about recklessness & abandoned
justice & white supremacy's ghost—& this is
why I hate it all, the protests & their counters,

the Civil Rights attorneys that stalk the bodies
of the murdered, this dance of ours that reduces
humanity to the dichotomy of the veil. We are

not permitted to articulate the reasons we might
yearn to see a man die. A mind may abandon
sanity. What if all I had stomach for was blood?

But my mind is no sieve & sanity is no elixir
& I am bound to be haunted by the strength
that lets Tamir's father, mother, kinfolk resist

the temptation to turn everything they see
into a grave & make home the series of cells
that so many brothers already call their tomb.

Repetition Compulsion

You were telling the story, and suddenly
one of the characters was African American
as if none of the others had race;

as if race belongs first to one and then
by necessity to everyone; as if race hadn't been
what we were speaking all along.

You were telling a story, and still it isn't clear
what race is supposed to mean; so,
I turn to the listener who is also

the speaker and also a character
in this story, asking what to make of race
between people, and what to make

of the violence and excitements possible now that
race waits in the attention people share.

It would tell us its story about the mind
we are always inscribing, mind speaking
itself as attention, one of us noticing

the African American and the other
noticing but not noticing the implications
beyond one story about race, beyond

a character not much of a mind except
in response to being minded.
But we don't speak the histories still

resisting inscription; our sudden foreclosure?—
mindlessness in the American story
we are going and are going to repeat.

ode to my blackness

you are my shelter from the storm
                    and the storm

my anchor

                and the troubled sea

                    *   *   *

night casts you warm and glittering
upon my shoulders   some would
say you give off no heat   some folks
can't see beyond the closest star

                    *   *   *

you are the tunnel john henry died
            to carve
i see the light
            at the end   of you   the beginning

                    *   *   *

i dig down deep and there you are   are at the root of my blues
you're all thick and dark, enveloping   the root of my blues
seem like it's so hard to let you go   when i got   nothing   to lose

                    *   *   *

without you, i would be just

        a self of my former shadow

Ode to My Whiteness

after Evie Shockley

You were invisible to me.
You went without saying.
You were my weapon secret from myself.
Whatever I got, you helped get it for me.
You were my ignorance.
Because of you I was not innocent.
I did not see that—you were my blinding light.
My dreams had a blank area in the center,
taking up most of the screen they played on in my sleep—
a blazing circle that blanked out the core of the scene.
I thought it was my mother's violence,
but it was you, too.
You the unseen fat which fed me in the wilderness.
You my masonic handshake.
You my stealth.
You my drone.
You my collaborator.
You my magician's cloak of steam,
you my dissembler.
You mine? I yours,
irisless eyeball, you my blindness,
inspiration of my helpless act,
you my silence. Evie's blackness
a dancer, you another, the two of you moving together.

American Sonnet for My Past and Future Assassin

Rilke ends his sonnet "Archaic Torso of Apollo" saying
"You must change your life." James Wright ends "Lying
In a Hammock at William Duffy's Farm in Pine Island,
Minnesota" saying "I have wasted my life." Ruth Stone ends
"A Moment" saying "You do not want to repeat my life."
A minute seed with a giant soul kicking inside it at the end
And beginning of life. After the opening scene where
A car bomb destroys the black detective's family, there are
Several scenes of our hero at the edge of life. A shootout
In an African American Folk Museum, a shootout
In the middle of an interstate rest stop parking lot, a shootout
In a barn endangering the farm life. The life
That burns a hole through life, that leaves a scar for life,
That makes you weep for another life. Define *life*.

Conjure Fire

To begin:
braid the wick at dawn,
so it learns
strength in glowing,
its own brief history.

Keep the tallow near sand,
on the top shelf,
rarely visited,
in case all the bulbs fail,
as if a handful
can make us remember
how big the ocean,
how far the shore.

Be patient as wax
becomes liquid, solid,
again liquid when
we start to measure
time in gone inches.

The weather will come;
the sun will leave.
We make our own light
when we need to.

from *The Tempest,* Act I, Scene ii

PROSPERO

    We'll visit Caliban, my slave, who never

    Yields us kind answer. . . . But as 'tis,

    We cannot miss him: he does make our fire,

    Fetch in our wood, and serves in offices

    That profit us. What ho! slave! Caliban! . . .

    Thou poisonous slave, got by the devil himself

    Upon thy wicked dam, come forth!

CALIBAN

    As wicked dew as e'er my mother brushed

    With raven's feather from unwholesome fen

    Drop on you both! . . .

    This island's mine by Sycorax my mother,

    Which thou tak'st from me. . . .

PROSPERO   Thou most lying slave,

    Whom stripes may move, not kindness! I have used thee

    (Filth as thou art) with humane care, and lodged thee

    In mine own cell. . . .

MIRANDA   Abhorrèd slave, . . . I pitied thee,

    Took pains to make thee speak, taught thee each hour

    One thing or another: when thou didst not, savage,

    Know thine own meaning, but wouldst gabble like

    A thing most brutish, I endowed thy purposes

    With words that made them known. But thy vile race,

    Though thou didst learn, had that in't which good natures

    Could not abide to be with. . . .

CALIBAN

    You taught me language, and my profit on't

    Is, I know how to curse. The red plague rid you

    For learning me your language!

from *Voyage of the Sable Venus*, Catalog 4

At Auction Negro Man in Loincloth
serves liquor to Men Bidding

on The Slaves while A Slave Woman
attends Two Women Observing The Sale.

African Slave Encased in an Iron Mask
and Collar Slave Children starting out

to harvest coffee on an oxcart.
Negroes under a date palm.

Negro Woman Seated
at a table, facing

left, writing
with a quill.

America Gives Its Blackness Back to Me

The shadow I had carried lightly has
Been forced upon me now and heavy since

Bulky since   now and since unwieldy as
A corpse the shadow I   was born from in

And to I   should have known I couldn't being
As how it wasn't me who lifted it

Not   all the way   from me in the first place being
As how its lightness after was a gift

Its near-   bodilessness a gift   from those
Who bind it to me now I should have known

I couldn't while they watched me   set it loose
They bind it   to my back they make it strange
That I knew   in my arms they weigh it down

With the shadow they had kept the bindings in

Mess Hall

Your knives tip down
in the dish rack
of the replica plantation home,
you wash hands

with soap pressed into seahorses
and scallop shells white
to match your guest towels,
and, like an escargot fork, America,

you have found the dimensions
small enough to break a man—
a wet rag,

a bullet, a bullet
like a bishop,
or an armless knight
of the Ku Klux Klan,

the silhouette
through your nighttime window,
a quarter
plays a song you admire,

outside, a ring of concertina wire
circles around a small collapse.
America, ignore the window and look at your lap:
even your dinner napkins are on FIRE.

NEGRO BAPTIST CHURCH, LOGANVILLE, GA, 1947: ST. JAMES AME CHURCH, LAKE CITY,

SC, 1955: PINE GROVE AME CHURCH, SUMMERTON, SC, 1955: NEW HOPE BAPTIST

CHURCH, CLEVELAND, MS, 1957: I HOPE BAPTIST CHURCH, COLQUITT, GA, 1962:

Jubilee Blues
(choral)

Once burst loose from human bondage,
do our songs still tow our pain like a mule?
Tell me, if we done burst loose from bondage,
do our songs still carry hurt like a mule?
They haul thundered oceans of auction blocks
homeward, pulling our lost cargo through.
If this freight of psalm should hit a rock
we're gonna do just what the old folk do.
If this load of song ever strike on rock
we gone do what we was born to do—
gone pull a whole lot harder—ain't gone stop
till all of heaven bleeds out of blue.
Every time we split our mouths to song,
we'll bind the air with hallelujah's bond.

HIGH HOPE BAPTIST CHURCH, DAWSON, GA, 1962: MOUNT OLIVE BAPTIST CHURCH,

ALBANY, GA, 1962: MOUNT MARY BAPTIST CHURCH, ALBANY, GA, 1962: ST. MATTHEW'S

BAPTIST CHURCH, MACON, GA, 1962: SHADY GROVE BAPTIST CHURCH, ALBANY, GA, 1962:

Frederick Douglass

When it is finally ours, this freedom, this liberty, this beautiful
and terrible thing, needful to man as air,
usable as earth; when it belongs at last to all,
when it is truly instinct, brain matter, diastole, systole,
reflex action; when it is finally won; when it is more
than the gaudy mumbo jumbo of politicians:
this man, this Douglass, this former slave, this Negro
beaten to his knees, exiled, visioning a world
where none is lonely, none hunted, alien,
this man, superb in love and logic, this man
shall be remembered. Oh, not with statues' rhetoric,
not with legends and poems and wreaths of bronze alone,
but with the lives grown out of his life, the lives
fleshing his dream of the beautiful, needful thing.

The Fool's Song

Another Reason

The sky is always dark blue, trending toward lavender
when I remember and say *we should not go extinct*,
and each time this knowledge arrives
like a silent taxi headlamp in the rain.

This evening it comes in a black and white video
of Grigory Sokolov playing a Bach partita,
his soft white hair shining out of the preponderant dark
as he hunches over the piano keys,
his hands up and down, one after another,
each like a falcon rising
through its precisely hollowed wind
then falling, falling to its prey.
His rounded shoulders
enact the geometry he long ago committed to
in secret prayer. The odd, old
bulk of him, the sweet mild eyebrows,
speak of books and candles;
but here is the orchard again (with its dark blue scent
of rain and lavender) coming up so close beside the house.

On Setting a Migrant Goose Free

Snows heavy at Hsan-yang this tenth-year winter,
river water spawns ice, tree branches break and fall,

and hungry birds flock east and west by the hundred,
a migrant goose crying starvation loudest among them.

Pecking through snow for grass, sleeping nights on ice,
its cold wings lumber slower and slower up into flight,

and soon it's tangled in a river boy's net, carried away
snug in his arms, and put for sale alive in the market.

Once a man of the north, I'm accused and exiled here.
Man and bird, though different, we're both visitors,

and it hurts a visiting man to see a visiting bird's pain,
so I pay the ransom and set you free. Goose, o soaring

goose, rising into clouds—where will you fly now?
Don't fly northwest, that's the last place you should go.

There in Huai-hsi, rebels still loose, there's no peace,
just a million armored soldiers long massed for battle:

imperial and rebel armies grown old facing each other.
Starved and exhausted, they'd love to get hold of you,

those soldiers. They'd shoot you down and have a feast
then pluck your wings clean to feather their arrows.

Translated by David Hinton

A Message to Po Chü-i

In that tenth winter of your exile
the cold never letting go of you
and your hunger aching inside you
day and night while you heard the voices
out of the starving mouths around you
old ones and infants and animals
those curtains of bones swaying on stilts
and you heard the faint cries of the birds
searching in the frozen mud for something
to swallow and you watched the migrants
trapped in the cold the great geese growing
weaker by the day until their wings
could barely lift them above the ground
so that a gang of boys could catch one
in a net and drag him to market
to be cooked and it was then that you
saw him in his own exile and you
paid for him and kept him until he
could fly again and you let him go
but then where could he go in the world
of your time with its wars everywhere
and the soldiers hungry the fires lit
the knives out twelve hundred years ago

I have been wanting to let you know
the goose is well he is here with me
you would recognize the old migrant
he has been with me for a long time
and is in no hurry to leave here
the wars are bigger now than ever
greed has reached numbers that you would not
believe and I will not tell you what
is done to geese before they kill them
now we are melting the very poles
of the earth but I have never known
where he would go after he leaves me

The Pillory and the Steepled Dark

after Joseph Wright's 1768 painting,
An Experiment on a Bird in the Air Pump

The suffocating cockatoo falls limp
inside a glass vacuum-bowl, its feathers
upturned and splayed from breathless panicking.
Its broad breast grays in candlelight, like snow
around a bonfire where ashes mist
to cloak its sheen. Why not call this science
in 1768, this crowded room
of villagers who left their creaky dens
to plod with invitations scribbled down
beyond the pillory and the steepled dark:
the widower who instantly regrets
he brought his dainty daughters to recoil,
a pair of lovers young enough to need
a ruse to meet, the despondent poet
staring at a skull submerged in ooze,
and two apprentices, prim and dapper,
who dutifully mark each second's tick?
The amateur philosopher stares out
disheveled and amazed, feeling finally
the derangement of a god, the awful dream
his machinery contains. His weary son
hoists the empty cage back to the ceiling,
tugging gingerly at the pulley rope
that squeaks till taut. A boy knows how this ends.
He's seen resurrections work their spell
until no flood of air can lift a wing.
There are no eager watchers then, behind
the paint-chipped barn, when a sacrifice
is heaped into a sacrificial grave
he opens with the moonlight on his spade.

The Fool's Song

I tried to put a bird in a cage.
    O fool that I am!
     For the bird was Truth.
Sing merrily, Truth: I tried to put
    Truth in a cage!

And when I had the bird in the cage,
    O fool that I am!
    Why, it broke my pretty cage.
Sing merrily, Truth: I tried to put
    Truth in a cage!

And when the bird was flown from the cage,
    O fool that I am!
    Why, I had nor bird nor cage.
Sing merrily, Truth: I tried to put
    Truth in a cage!
    Heigh-ho! Truth in a cage.

April 14, 2017: Reading the News

Trump's EPA Chief Scott Pruitt Calls for an Exit to the Paris Climate Agreement

This morning I see that 100 men in suits are willing to throw away the world so they can have more small green rectangles made from trees.

It's spring. Plum blossoms speckle the sidewalk and fall on my shoes, flake after flake, but l can't forget these men, chopping away on the other side of my life.

I keep reminding myself l don't know how it's going is end. Attila scorched and divided. But the grass from those burnt blades grew over him.

The Right of the Strong

The right of the strong is to take everything.
Memory and youth, clouds and
melancholy. I didn't know,
I swear I didn't know what I was doing,
robbing all of you of your hearts. I was
just happy, moved and grateful to my
bright stars. I thought my loot was
love, and dust, mute now,
a gift. I raised many
species. Winged monkeys and
sky-blue cockatoos. Even you,
foxes, I lured over, so you became
the king among beasts. I truly thought I was
a holy ant that brought it all
on its own shoulders. Therefore now
I rot deliriously, waiting for the hour
you, meadows, will turn green. With
the erasure of my body the seal will be
returned to you. Crickets and brooks, sunrise
above the Trenta valley. The soft
mists above home will again be
sacred, as they used to be.
Just a while longer, poisoned children. Just
one more sip before I return
to earth.

Translated by Michael Biggins

Earth Day

Truth has gone, like Thoreau,
deep into the woods
to study water,
to study trees,
gone underground
to study peace
among the worms
and the mute moles,
to thrive in the silence
of earth with the good
dirt in her mouth,
tattered twigs in her lashes.
In this silence a kind of beauty
not found in the rattle above
that is like tin drums,
knives clanging.
She hears ants marching,
carrying the wounded,
harvesting the dead,
rabbits sheltered in warrens,
earth's rumbling like hunger
in the belly.
It is April. Bulbs push
through tangled roots.
Truth rests on her back
like an invalid with fevered
forehead, cold hands,
face turned toward
the light.

At Standing Rock

(A rhupunt)

The serpent comes.
Its black blood hums
As venom numbs
The lakes and land.

No treaties hold.
The white men sold
Their word for gold
Before they manned

The hungry drill
That pierced Black Hill.
Soon oil will fill
The veins law banned.

They tunneled deep—
Black bile will seep
Where old bones sleep
In sacred sand.

At death, at birth,
Red feet kiss Earth.
Her life is worth
The flames we fanned

At Standing Rock,
Our bodies block
The fangs that lock
On Mother's hand.

Our home we hold
Despite the cold.
We will not fold
On rocks that stand.

why humans?

for the joke, even the pun,
for black humor in a bleak hour,
for the complication of stuff: tangled,
woven, manufactured, compressed, crooked,
cooked, plastic and rubber and Corian,
concrete, steel, and asphalt,
for glass blown
from sand and fire,
for grammar, for the 6,500 spoken languages,
for *mensch* and *derriere* and *giggle* and *preposterous*,
for the winch, the pulley, the level, the wheel,
for faucets that turn on when you wave your hand,
for hands, for their cunning thumbs,
for false teeth,
false testimony, avarice,
compassion, for the known step
of the beloved on the stairs,
eyebrow and gap tooth, elfin ear,
for arrival, for departure,
the longing for return,
for the embrace,
the howl, the song,
for the brief spark
in the spiraling
dark

The City

You said: "I'll go to another country, go to another shore,
find another city better than this one.
Whatever I try to do is fated to turn out wrong
and my heart lies buried like something dead.
How long can I let my mind moulder in this place?
Wherever I turn, wherever I look,
I see the black ruins of my life, here,
where I've spent so many years, wasted them, destroyed them totally."

You won't find a new country, won't find another shore.
This city will always pursue you.
You'll walk the same streets, grow old
in the same neighborhoods, turn gray in these same houses.
You'll always end up in this city. Don't hope for things elsewhere:
there's no ship for you, there's no road.
Now that you've wasted your life here, in this small corner,
you've destroyed it everywhere in the world.

Translated by Edmund Keeley and Philip Sherrard

Shine, Perishing Republic

While this America settles in the mould of its vulgarity, heavily
    thickening to empire,
And protest, only a bubble in the molten mass, pops and sighs out,
    and the mass hardens,

I sadly smiling remember that this flower fades to make fruit, the
    fruit rots to make earth.
Out of the mother; and through the spring exultances, ripeness
    and decadence; and home to the mother.

You making haste haste on decay: not blameworthy; life is good,
    be it stubbornly long or suddenly
A mortal splendor: meteors are not needed less than mountains:
    shine, perishing republic.

But for my children, I would have them keep their distance from
    the thickening center; corruption
Never has been compulsory, when the cities lie at the monster's
    feet there are left the mountains.

And boys, be in nothing so moderate as in love of man, a clever
    servant, insufferable master.
There is the trap what catches noblest spirits, that caught—they
    say—God, when he walked on earth.

National Politics

Even though we watch every year
as the snow melts and runs along ditches
and gutters, finds the low places,
enters the creeks and the culverts, fanning
out wider to cover the gravel of rivers,
washing mud from the banks, testing
the bridges, splashing, tumbling granite,

even when crocuses push their green
crowns through the leaf mold, the succulent
not-quite-spring muck, and then open,
flashing the earliest colors, and mornings
inch their way upward by the half-minute
and evenings last just a notch longer,
barely perceptibly stretching the days,

we still can't believe it, we're sure every winter
will hold us forever, that hoping is useless.

Sun Bear

yesterday at the Oakland zoo
I was walking alone for a moment
past the enclosure holding the sun bear
also known as beruang madu
it looked at me without interest
it has powerful jaws and truly loves honey
it sleeps in a high hammock
its claws look made out of wood
and if it dreams at all it is of Malaysia
home of its enemy the clouded leopard
a gorgeous arboreal
hunting and eating machine
whose coat resembles a python
now it is night and the zoo is closed
some animals are sleeping
the nocturnals moving in their cages
getting ready to hunt nothing
I don't know why but I feel sure
something has woken the sun bear
it is awake in the dark
maybe it is my spirit animal
I am reading about the early snow
that has fallen on the Northeast
all the power shutting down
the weather going insane
the animals cannot help us
they go on moving without love
though we look into their eyes and feel
sure we see it there and maybe
we are right nothing
can replace animal love
not even complicated human love
we sometimes choose to allow
ourselves to be chosen by
despite what everyone knows

the problem is
in order to love anything
but an animal you cannot allow
yourself to believe in those things
that are if we don't stop them
going to destroy us

These Strangers in a Foreign World

No. 1096

These Strangers, in a foreign World,
Protection asked of me—
Befriend them, lest Yourself in Heaven
Be found a Refugee—

The Departure from Fallen Troy

from Aeneid *(Book II, lines 692–719)*

As he spoke we could hear, ever more loudly, the noise
Of the burning fires; the flood of flames was coming
Nearer and nearer. "My father, let me take you
Upon my shoulders and carry you with me.
The burden will be easy. Whatever happens,
You and I will experience it together,
Peril or safety, whichever it will be.
Little Iülus will come along beside me.
My wife will follow behind us. And you, my servants,
Listen to what I say: just as you leave
The limits of the city there is a mound,
And the vestiges of a deserted temple of Ceres,
And a cypress tree that has been preserved alive
For many years by the piety of our fathers.
We will all meet there, though perhaps by different ways
And, father, you must carry in your arms
The holy images of our household gods;
I, coming so late from the fighting and the carnage
Cannot presume to touch them until I have washed
Myself in running water." Thus I spoke.

I take up the tawny pelt of a lion and
Cover my neck and my broad shoulders with it,
And bowing down, I accept the weight of my father;
Iülus puts his hand in mine and goes
Along beside me, trying to match my steps
As best he can, trying his best to keep up.
My wife follows behind us, a little way back.
So we all set out together, making our way. . . .

Translated by David Ferry

Dear Exile,

Never step back   Never a last
Scent of plumeria

When my parents left
You knew it was for good

    It's a herd of horses never
        To reclaim their   steppes

You became a moth hanging
Down from the sun

Old river   Calling to my mother
Kept spilling out of her lungs

Ridgeline vista closed
Into the locket of their gaze

      It's the Siberian crane
    Forbidden   to fly back after winter

You marbled my father's face
Floated him as stone over the sea

Further   Every minute
Emptying his child years to the land

You crawled back in your bomb

    It's when the banyan must leave
Relearn to cathedral its roots

The Mercy

The ship that took my mother to Ellis Island
eighty-three years ago was named "The Mercy."
She remembers trying to eat a banana
without first peeling it and seeing her first orange
in the hands of a young Scot, a seaman
who gave her a bite and wiped her mouth for her
with a red bandana and taught her the word,
"orange," saying it patiently over and over.
A long autumn voyage, the days darkening
with the black waters calming as night came on,
then nothing as far as her eyes could see and space
without limit rushing off to the corners
of creation. She prayed in Russian and Yiddish
to find her family in New York, prayers
unheard or misunderstood or perhaps ignored
by all the powers that swept the waves of darkness
before she woke, that kept "The Mercy" afloat
while smallpox raged among the passengers
and crew until the dead were buried at sea
with strange prayers in a tongue she could not fathom.
"The Mercy," I read on the yellowing pages of a book
I located in a windowless room of the library
on 42nd Street, sat thirty-one days
offshore in quarantine before the passengers
disembarked. There a story ends. Other ships
arrived, "Tancred" out of Glasgow, "The Neptune"
registered as Danish, "Umberto IV,"
the list goes on for pages, November gives
way to winter, the sea pounds this alien shore.
Italian miners from Piemonte dig
under towns in western Pennsylvania
only to rediscover the same nightmare
they left at home. A nine-year-old girl travels

all night by train with one suitcase and an orange.
She learns that mercy is something you can eat
again and again while the juice spills over
your chin, you can wipe it away with the back
of your hands and you can never get enough.

Blad

He said: "It was a country then."

And by *country*, he meant that the sky rained water
not shrapnel.

That the earth grew cedars, not teetering
columns.

All that is left of the buildings.

That their neighbors came over for tea
unmasked, gunless.

He said: "The whole family would go to the shore. Deck the sand with barbecue pits, the men
falling in rows to play the durbakkeh by the waterline.

Now they are dumping the bodies in the sea. No place to bury them
they said.

Why don't they bury them in the desert?

The desert is so vast

and can hold so many bodies."

I have no answers for his question. Conversations like these are one-sided.

And what could I have said? That perhaps overwhelming death coupled with persistent threat
necessitates a quickness the rushing of the waves provides?

The sea is a place that is somewhere—*there*, beyond the waterline. That is precisely why the
others are leaving. Why your parents have left.

Here, on this side of the waterline, is nowhere.

The Baggage

Prepare your baggage
leave everything heavy
      whatever might be an obstacle to your feet along the trails
Light as a feather you must leave
to leap   to fly

Pack your bags for good
leave the pain here
      with me to look after
leave the yearning
      so it does not sicken you there.

But do not forget to carry
the gift of the tiger
      to withstand the trails
the gift of the eagle
      so that no hand may stop you
You must return to the place which preserves your umbilical cord

Translated by Donald Stang

"You shall leave behind all you most dearly love"

from Paradiso *(Canto XVII, lines 43–69)*

"And thus, as harmony's sweet sound may rise
  from mingled voices to the ear. So rises to my sight
  a vision of the time that lies in store for you.

"As Hippolytus was forced to flee from Athens,
  because of his stepmother, treacherous and fierce,
  so shall you be forced to flee from Florence.

"This is the plan, already set in motion,
  that soon will bring success to him who plots it
  where Christ is bought and sold all day.

"The populace shall blame the injured party,
  as it always does, but vengeance
  shall bear witness to the Truth that metes it out.

"You shall leave behind all you most dearly love,
  and that shall be the arrow
  first loosed from exile's bow.

"You shall learn how salt is the taste
  of another man's bread and how hard is the way,
  going down and then up, another man's stairs.

"But the heaviest burden your shoulders must bear
  shall be the companions, wicked and witless,
  among whom you shall fall in your descent.

"They, utterly ungrateful, mad, and faithless
  shall turn against you. But soon enough they, not you,
  shall feel their faces blushing past their brows.

"Of their brutish state the results
  shall offer proof. And it shall bring you honor
  to have made a single party of yourself alone."

Translated by Robert Hollander and Jean Hollander

The New Colossus

Not like the brazen giant of Greek fame,
With conquering limbs astride from land to land;
Here at our sea-washed, sunset gates shall stand
A mighty woman with a torch, whose flame
Is the imprisoned lightning, and her name
Mother of Exiles. From her beacon-hand
Glows world-wide welcome; her mild eyes command
The air-bridged harbor that twin cities frame.
"Keep, ancient lands, your storied pomp!" cries she
With silent lips. "Give me your tired, your poor,
Your huddled masses yearning to breathe free,
The wretched refuse of your teeming shore.
Send these, the homeless, tempest-tossed to me,
I lift my lamp beside the golden door!"

That Damned Fence

Anonymous poem circulated at the Poston Internment Camp

They've sunk the posts deep into the ground,
They've strung out wires all the way around.
With machine gun nests just over there,
And sentries and soldiers everywhere.

We're trapped like rats in a wired cage,
To fret and fume with impotent rage;
Yonder whispers the lure of the night,
But that DAMNED FENCE assails our sight.

We seek the softness of the midnight air,
But that DAMNED FENCE in the floodlight glare
Awakens unrest in our nocturnal quest,
And mockingly laughs with vicious jest.

With nowhere to go and nothing to do,
We feel terrible, lonesome, and blue:
That DAMNED FENCE is driving us crazy,
Destroying our youth and making us lazy.

Imprisoned in here for a long, long time,
We know we're punished—though we've committed no crime,
Our thoughts are gloomy and enthusiasm damp,
To be locked up in a concentration camp.

Loyalty we know, and patriotism we feel,
To sacrifice our utmost was our ideal,
To fight for our country, and die, perhaps;
But we're here because we happen to be Japs.

We all love life, and our country best,
Our misfortune to be here in the west,
To keep us penned behind that DAMNED FENCE,
Is someone's notion of NATIONAL DEFENCE!

"The East-West border . . ."

The East-West border is always wandering,
sometimes eastward, sometimes west,
and we do not know exactly where it is just now:
in Gaugamela, in the Urals, or maybe in ourselves,
so that one ear, one eye, one nostril, one hand, one foot,
one lung and one testicle or one ovary
is on the one, another on the other side. Only the heart,
only the heart is always on one side:
if we are looking northward, in the West;
if we are looking southward, in the East;
and the mouth doesn't know on behalf of which or both
it has to speak.

Translated by the author with Sam Hamill and Riina Tamm

Disciple

Farouk lifted the old Cadillac up onto 80 going west
pulled a cigarette from the breast pocket of his denim shirt
though as a practicing Muslim he does not smoke
but the road is an addiction the Koran does not forbid
and the jobs he quit and the books he's read were kindling
so now the flame inside burns no color and no religion
just one man trying to escape his plight by believing in the promise
here on the faded yet still fecund stones of home

Growing Up a Halfie

It is never admitting you've been to a bullfight.
It is knowing Carlos Santana's old-school jams were tighter
        than his new sell-out riffs.
It was my mom teaching me that Mexico had the first socialist revolution
          but it was me deferring to Marx so I could sleep with the coed
              who studied 20th-century history.
It is the mango versus the pear.
It is secretly watching soccer matches wearing an Aztecan jersey.
It is the Zapata image next to the George Washington image.
It is the language fighting the image, taunting the idea, that
        makes me silent and loud at the same instant.
It is the history of ritual sacrifices next to the history of genocide.
It is thinking in different languages, then going to sleep
        and waking up with ideas you know you'll never say.
It is the burro over the hot dog,
       but it is apple pie over flan.
It is turkey in November and menudo in December.
It is the border moving at night
And me moving over the border at will.
It is an invisible line that runs over my body.

Another Damascus in Damascus

Another Damascus in Damascus, an eternal one.
I was unfair to you, friend, when you criticized my migration to a heartbeat.
Now it's my right, now after my return, to ask you in friendship:
Why did you lean on a dagger to look at me?
Why did you raise up my slopes even higher
so that my horses may fall on me?
I had hoped to carry you to the gushing spring
of the ode, to the ends of the earth. What a beauty you are!
What a beauty is Damascus if it were not for my wounds.
So let one half of your heart, friend, join one half of mine.
Let us create a strong and farseeing heart for her, for me, for you.
For another Damascus to mirror my soul in Damascus.

Translated by Munir Akash and Carolyn Forché

Executive Order

SUSANNA LANG

When a man is held at the airport
because our borders closed while his plane was still in the air,

the tumblers in our locks fall out of alignment
and our front doors refuse entrance to our keys.

When the man held at the airport is not allowed to speak with a lawyer
the keys break off in our back doors.

There are no locksmiths available
though we call every number we can find.

When the man's son stirs in his sleep, sixteen hundred miles away
from the airport where his father now waits for a return flight,

our first-floor windows paint themselves shut,
and wrought-iron bars install themselves over the glass.

When the man is put on a plane back to the place
where officials wait to escort him to prison,

we sit on our front stoops, the January wind finding the skin
where our sleeves do not quite meet our gloves.

Home to Roost

Money

Someone had the idea of getting more water
released beneath the Don Pedro Dam
into the once-green Tuolumne,—

so the minnows could have some wiggle room,
so the salmon could lunge far enough up
to spawn, so that there would be more salmon

in the more water below the dam.
But it wasn't possible—by then the water
didn't belong to the salmon anymore, by then

the water didn't even belong to the river.
The water didn't belong to the water.

London

I wander thro' each charter'd street,
Near where the charter'd Thames does flow,
And mark in every face I meet
Marks of weakness, marks of woe.

In every cry of every man,
In every Infant's cry of fear,
In every voice, in every ban,
The mind-forg'd manacles I hear.

How the Chimney-sweeper's cry
Every blackning Church appalls;
And the hapless Soldier's sigh
Runs in blood down Palace walls.

But most thro' midnight streets I hear
How the youthful Harlot's curse
Blasts the new-born Infant's tear,
And blights with plagues the Marriage hearse.

About the Money

When they say it's not about the money,
it's about the money.
— *ANONYMOUS*

By the turn of the century
Talking about the money
Replaced talking about the sex,

Talking about one's so-called
Religious life, and all that
Earlier yak about the psyche.

Talking about the money
Got down to it and captured
The hunger, the hope,

The love, and the fear:
Let me hear your money talk,
Many sang.

Money was a good time
(What people want most is
Good times and insurance?)

And money picked up
The garbage the following
Morning. (Someone's

Got to do it and someone gets
Money to *do it*.) There was
Really nothing like talking

About the money if you wanted
To really get to know someone,
To get to know what animated,

What moved the American.
Do me. Do it to me, honey.
Do my money. Let's get cynical:

Let me hear your money talk.

GOMER [*]

Back again . . . *talkin' about heaven* . . . No blood, no pus. This old fellow sleeps in doorways. Dirty as hell. Says we voted for hell, so he needs the laying on of hands. Bright lights. Voices soft as his mother's . . . *talkin' about leavin' but not going there* . . . Juice and Jell-O. Crackers. Feet washed, swabbed with soothing lotion. Not ready for the Jesus Bus, yet singing . . . *got shoes for walkin' to heaven.* . . . And says this maybe-president may be walkin' the other way. No Greyhound Therapy for this weekly GOMER. No Freud Squad. Instead, we let him go in clean scrubs with a new blanket and twenty bucks, which may get him and us closer to God's heaven.

*GOMER is an emergency room acronym for "Get Out of My Emergency Room," used for patients who return there again and again.

An Augury

Caligula, son of Germanicus, gave the people
circuses. Winners, losers, gore. When bored
at gladiator games, he'd order front-row Romans
tossed in. The crowd, stunned, roared.

His infrastructure projects—job creators—
aqueducts, palaces, walls—drained the Treasury.
Pleasure barges *al lago* bore his name, weighted
with gilded suites, gardens, marble colonnades.

A granite obelisk, plunder from Egypt,
towered, reconstructed, at the center of Rome.
Limbic impulse led him. No senator's
wife was safe from banquet-table groping.

Treason trials thinned imagined enemies.
Caligula's unmet needs ginned up,
demanding temple-god beheadings.
His marble likenesses replaced the pantheon.

Sleepless, he wandered his massive
white palace on the Palatine Hill
conversing with Jupiter or the moon.
He wallowed in piles of shiny coins.

A hairy man, unshapely.
To mention a goat was a capital offense.
Critics—*public enemies*—were torn to pieces,
bowels dragged through streets and heaped before him.

Three years, ten months, eight days—
an emperor tilted at conspiracies.
We have this from Dios and Suetonius.
Writers, historians, theirs are the words that lasted.

Rome teetered until the Senate turned
and the republic, ragged beast, stumbled on.

Ballad of the Indivisible

We're mashing up the believable and the inconceivable,
thrashing through this trash for whatever is retrievable.
Do we need to do consider this wretchedness relievable
any day now? And how.

I don't like—I love—whatever is bearable,
but that cloak of doom, darling, is simply unwearable.
Do we need to make room for the wildly cheerable
and true? Yeah, we do.

The troubadour of erotic despair is no more,
but the songs he once launched from an amorous shore
have reached 'round the world, a world always at war
with death. Deep breath . . .

Now follow up the phone calls and emails sent
with the colors that broadcast your awesome intent
and declare to all those who are said to represent:
We're here. And not going anywhere.

Yeah, it's maddening a con man can unconscionably sell
a hateful bill of goods that's straight out of hell.
But if I have to dumpster dive through this deplorable smell
for sweet liberty, I'm glad it's with thee.

We who resist this nefarious fuss
will never throw each other under the bus.
We pledge allegiance to the republic of us,
our soul-deep endeavor. Forever.

American Wars

Like the topaz in the toad's head
the comfort in the terrible histories
was up front, easy to find:
Once upon a time in a kingdom far away.

Even to the dreadful now of news
we listened comforted
by far time-zones, language we didn't speak,
the wide, forgetful oceans.

Today, no comfort but the jewel courage.
The war is ours, now, here, it is our republic
facing its own betraying terror.
And how we tell the story is forever after.

Coast Starlight

Out of the station. Out of the rail-yard's braiding
and unbraiding tracks. Onto the one track
skimming the edge of the coast's flat gray water.
On one side, marinas and houseboats
and the demolished timber mills' supports, sticking out
of the water like burned matchsticks.
On the other side the crumbling spread of landscape.
Woods. Little Woods where there are as many trees
toppled over as there are live ones. Moss
on everything an earnest green fuzz. The ferns deeply
wet, then the junk in the poor yards behind
factories, trailers, houses. Morning, and the light is
the day's information.
                          What was I talking about,
talking about the place of the political
in poems, the students writing down what I said
to them. That you have to keep distressing the canvas
of the personal. That you need to ask what is
left out for beauty's sake, to see how the unspoken
will inflect the things you have allowed yourself to say.
Now these marshy places. Grasses and cattails,
which are not caricatures of knowledge.
Pools of milky green water. And the creeks curving
into sudden sight like a heartache. The mind going
over and over things, not knowing what to do
with the world but to turn it into something else.

Kara Walker's Sphinx

*This creature is a power image, a
colossal goddess of the future . . . a blind
diviner who knows that the American
future is much less white, racially, than
its past.*
—THE NEW YORK TIMES

She crouches near the East River
in a defunct sugar refinery:
the riddler
and the riddle.

Her forebears—
sentinels on temple step, on Theban road—
watched the rise of millennial suns,
the rise of pyramids,
freighted with foreign bondage.

One remained
and saw the fall
of temple and pharaoh,
their melt into Egyptian sand.

Here in an abandoned
Brooklyn warehouse
still redolent of Caribbean cane—
a modern sphinx waits.

May it not take a millennium
for this temple to fall.
(This factory's fate is sure:
condos will rise here.)

It is her privilege now:
we must answer her—
we have much
to answer for.

When the Saints Come Marching In

Plentiful sacrifice and believers in redemption
are all that is needed
so any day now
I expect
some new religion
to rise up like tear gas
from the streets of New York
erupting like the rank pavement smell
released by a garbage truck's
baptismal drizzle.

High priests are ready and waiting
their incense pans full of fire.
I do not know the rituals
the exhalations
nor what name of the god
the survivors will worship
I only know she will be terrible
and very busy
and very old.

The Second Coming

Turning and turning in the widening gyre
The falcon cannot hear the falconer;
Things fall apart; the centre cannot hold;
Mere anarchy is loosed upon the world,
The blood-dimmed tide is loosed, and everywhere
The ceremony of innocence is drowned;
The best lack all conviction, while the worst
Are full of passionate intensity.

Surely some revelation is at hand;
Surely the Second Coming is at hand.
The Second Coming! Hardly are those words out
When a vast image out of *Spiritus Mundi*
Troubles my sight: somewhere in sands of the desert
A shape with lion body and the head of a man,
A gaze blank and pitiless as the sun,
Is moving its slow thighs, while all about it
Reel shadows of the indignant desert birds.
The darkness drops again; but now I know
That twenty centuries of stony sleep
Were vexed to nightmare by a rocking cradle,
And what rough beast, its hour come round at last,
Slouches towards Bethlehem to be born?

Home to Roost

The chickens
are circling and
blotting out the
day. The sun is
bright, but the
chickens are in
the way. Yes,
the sky is dark
with chickens,
dense with them.
They turn and
then they turn
again. These
are the chickens
you let loose
one at a time
and small—
various breeds.
Now they have
come home
to roost—all
the same kind
at the same speed.

Jade Flower Palace

The stream swirls. The wind moans in
The pines. Gray rats scurry over
broken tiles. What prince, long ago,
Built this palace standing in
Ruins beside the cliffs? There are
Green ghost fires in the black rooms.
The shattered pavements are all
Washed away. Ten thousand organ
Pipes whistle and roar. The storm
Scatters the red autumn leaves.
His dancing girls are yellow dust.
Their painted cheeks have crumbled
Away. His gold chariots
And courtiers are gone. Only
A stone horse is left of his
Glory. I sit on the grass and
start a poem, but the pathos of
It overcomes me. The future
Slips imperceptibly away.
Who can say what the years will bring?

Translated by Kenneth Rexroth

America, I Do Not Call Your
Name Without Hope

from "Changing North America"

Having helped initiate
the liberators of Poland
Czeslaw Milosz said to a Harvard audience
that in every era
the task of the *inspired* poet
is to *transcend his paltry ego*
and remind *the soul of the people*
of the open space ahead.

His example—sorely needed—
of overcoming *the schism*
between the poet and the human family
was Walt Whitman
his simplicity and power of the word

but Whitman could never speak
to the whole of America
the way Mickiewicz or Milosz
could unite Poland
in the face of a foreign oppressor.

It was Whitman's fate
to address an America
at war with itself.

"I resist anything better than my own diversity"

from "Song of Myself," Section 16 (Leaves of Grass, 1855)

I am of old and young, of the foolish as much as the wise,
Regardless of others, ever regardful of others,
Maternal as well as paternal, a child as well as a man,
Stuffed with the stuff that is coarse, and stuffed with the stuff that is fine,

One of the great nations, the nation of many nations—the smallest
    the same and the largest the same,
[. . . .]
Of every hue and trade and rank, of every caste and religion,
Not merely of the New World but of Africa, Europe or Asia. . . .
    a wandering savage,
A farmer, mechanic, or artist. . . . a gentleman, sailor, physician or priest.

I resist anything better than my own diversity,
And breathe the air and leave plenty after me,
And am not stuck up and am in my place.

The moth and the fisheggs are in their place,
The suns I see and suns I cannot see are in their place,
The palpable is in its place and the impalpable is in its place.

won't you celebrate with me

won't you celebrate with me
what i have shaped into
a kind of life? i had no model.
born in babylon
both nonwhite and woman
what did i see to be except myself?
i made it up
here on this bridge between
starshine and clay,
my one hand holding tight
my other hand; come celebrate
with me that every day
something has tried to kill me
and has failed.

One week later in the strange

One week later in the strange   → *clifton*
exhilaration after Lucille's death

our eyes were bright as we received instructions,
lined up with all we were supposed to do.

Now seers, now grace notes, now anchors, now tellers,
now keepers and spreaders, now wide open arms,

the cold wind of generational shift
blew all around us, stinging our cheeks,

awakening us to the open space
now everywhere surrounding.

Ode to the Heart

heart let me more have pity on
    —*GERARD MANLEY HOPKINS*

It's late in the day and the old school's deserted
but the door's unlocked. The linoleum dips
and bulges, the halls have shrunk.
And I shiver for the child
who entered that brick building,
his small face looking out
from the hood of a woolen coat.

My father told me that when he was a boy
the Jews lived on one block, Italians another.
To get home he had to pass
through the forbidden territory.
He undid his belt and swung it wildly
as he ran, wind whistling
through the buckle. Heart
be praised: you wake every morning.
You cast yourself into the streets.

The Crossing

for Congregation Sha'ar Zahav, San Francisco

God did not lead us by the nearer way
when Pharaoh let the people go at last,
but roundabout, by way of the wilderness—

pillars of fire and cloud marking night and day—
to the edge of the flood tide—uncrossable and vast.
If God had led us by the nearer way,

we cried, *we wouldn't die here; let Egypt oppress
us as it will; let us return to the past.*
But we have come out, by way of the wilderness,

in fear; on faith; free now, because we say
we are free; no longer the unchosen, the outcast.
God did not lead us by the nearer way,

but into rising waters, which do not part unless,
with an outstretched arm, we step forward, and stand fast.
Roundabout, by way of the wilderness,

we have come, blessed with love, lesbian, gay,
or sanctified in ways of our own, to bless
our God, who did not lead us by the nearer way,
but roundabout, by way of the wilderness.

Beshalach, Exodus *13:17–17:16*

I Like It When We Sit in the Backyard

for Tatjana Gromača

I like it when we sit in the backyard
Among our neighbors and their noisy pets
Here in the city with no privacy
The smells of cooking wafting in the air
Children being scolded to come and eat
And later those haphazard strings of lights
With the moon above them, shining brightly
While we talk about things that never change
Like the greed of our public officials
And life in this impossible country
Music, laughter, sometimes an argument
Drifting toward us on the evening breeze
In the morning our wineglasses full of rain.

Veterans Day

My daughter's gone to march with her troop
amid the bands and bunting, flags snapping
to honor troops from wars old and new, and
though I pass, I recall old Pickering in the mill
grousing about grief flowing from above when
he told them he wouldn't be in to work —
"My daughter's marching in the parade and
by god I'm gonna watch her," chin tilted
in defiance, surrendering a day's pay two years
before money shipped all our jobs south.

That was on the finishing line, up a level
from our tenter frames, where Johnny No-Ears
let others heat lunches under the lights, where
someone forgot to punch a hole and chicken and
noodles exploded over the stacked yards, hung
from the beams and no one knew nothing 'bout
nothing, and Johnny kept tending his box traps
just outside the window from my station,
saying, let me know if one's inside, just like
in the funnies, pigeons for the fattening.

We Defy Augury

Reading the word *inauguration* for the hundredth time
In the news, I caught it carrying the word *augur* inside it.
Augur, as in the priest in ancient Rome who was asked
To interpret the behavior of birds as an indication
Of divine approval or disapproval of some action
Being considered by the state. I see him on a hillside
Of olive trees, straining to hear whether they were
Calling in the branches where they had gathered
Or were silent. And if they took wing, squinting
To count their number and determine what sort
Of birds they were. Then observing which direction
They were flying. Whatever the answers, we know now
The birds were only looking to their own survival,
Obeying their hunger and their need to mate,
Migrating if they sensed the seasons were turning
Against them. We know too that the augur was
Interpreting the birds' behavior based on what
He thought the emperor wanted to do in his heart
Of hearts, or because he'd been bribed to say that
What the birds were doing meant this or that.
We know now it was all a sham. The words the favored
Daughter whispered in her father's ear where he sat
On his throne were the very words he'd told her
He would like to hear, words that boded well for her
And for the birds that every autumn settled
In that olive orchard and were spared,
And for the augur walking back through the dark
Toward the glittering city, under his lucky stars.

Inauguration Day in the Galápagos

January 20, 2017

The forecast that morning said possible rain,
but the air was dry, the sky cloudy,
as our bus climbed the hill on Santa Cruz,
taking us to the Tortoise Ecological Reserve
at the top of the island. We passed corn,
sugarcane and coffee plantations, stands
of cedars, and ranches where scrawny
cattle grazed. At the Reserve we borrowed
clumsy rubber boots to lumber through
the muddy terrain where giant tortoises,
like smooth, ancient dome-shaped rocks,
munched on low-lying plants. We hiked
through a lava tube on our way back
to the visitor center, where small brown
finches hopped and flitted about the tables.
No one mentioned the inauguration.

In the afternoon, our ship headed for Plaza Sur,
and as we waited for Zodiacs to take us
to the island, the Mormon Tabernacle Choir
was singing, prelude to a second showing
of the inauguration. My turn to debark
came quickly, and I saw dark marine iguanas
and golden land ones basking side by side.
Sea lions played in the waves. A yellow
warbler perched on a shrub; a short-eared
owl hid beneath it. Red carpetweed
dotted with prickly pear cacti spread in all
directions. Flocks of shearwaters and petrels
flashed beneath cliffs as frigate birds
dove for fish. Back on the ship, I was later
told, a man had threatened to jump overboard
if they showed the inauguration again,
so they waited until he was safe on Plaza Sur
surrounded by iguanas, others charmed
by blue-footed boobies, and the insistent
surge of the imperiled, luminous sea.

Ordinary Psalm with a Four-Letter Word

A single porch light burns in the flooded trailer park
& I'm trying to imagine spring as an urgency

waking in these steep hillsides resurrected green,
branches leafing out in shy mantillas,

even in this boy apparently born a girl
as he guns his uncle's truck under Highway 1,

the overpass crowded with kids holding signs—
Immigration makes America great & *Am I next?*—

& the boy honks in unison because the scars
he bears are like a flock of plovers turning

their white wings black along the edge
of never having been. He parks in a field

of artichokes beside a wall & climbs onto
the cab's roof into a constant wind off the Pacific.

Shakes the can, before scrawling *R-E-A-P*
in giant block letters & I swear to God,

it's not lost on me, the chilling implication,
What you sow. But commuting to work past his tag

in this year of so much rain, so little truth or kindness,
I need a word to signify exactly what it should.

REAP—as in this boy, means *to harvest, to gather
beauty as it is*; he means *to take it in*.

England in 1819

An old, mad, blind, despised, and dying king;
Princes, the dregs of their dull race, who flow
Through public scorn—mud from a muddy spring;
Rulers who neither see, nor feel, nor know,
But leech-like to their fainting country cling,
Till they drop, blind in blood, without a blow;
A people starved and stabbed on the untilled field;
An army, which liberticide and prey
Makes as a two-edged sword to all who wield;
Golden and sanguine laws which tempt and slay;
Religion Christless, Godless—a book sealed;
A senate, time's worst statute, unrepealed—
Are graves from which a glorious phantom may
Burst, to illumine our tempestuous day.

The Morning's Story

A word has abolished another word
a book has issued orders
to burn another book
a morning established by the violence of language
has changed the morning
of people's coughing

Maggots attack the kernel
the kernel comes from dull valleys
from among dull crowds
the government finds its spokesman
cats and mice
have similar expressions

On the road in the sky
the armed forester examines
the sun that rumbles past
over the asphalt lake
he hears the sound of disaster
the untrammeled sound of a great conflagration

Translated by Bonnie S. McDougall and Chen Maiping

Chosen

Noah was a just man . . . and Noah walked with God.
          —GENESIS 6:9

Did Noah ask God, as they walked together, what about
the girls on the river path on his way to work, giggling in knots, loitering back from
     the first milking,
the men fishing in the brightening gray, the women building up the fires,
the mice and lizards starting at his tread, rustling to safety in vain,
the boys following him, calling his name, the younger ones wheedling for something
     sweet, the bolder imitating his walk,
the walk of a man being careful not to seem pleased with himself—

did he remember, years and years ago, how the girls looked at him and did he still
     have affection for the cover of certain trees, in their last leaves now, with their
     prescient birds, shaken in an ill wind?

Or did he just squat without a word and scratch down 300 x 50 x 30 cubits, start
     sketching the window here so high, the door here,
sucking his teeth at the length of the keel, the draught so many times deeper than
     the river would bear—how was he going to explain that?

Could he already feel himself riding steadily upward on the waters, looking down at
     the people clinging to the oars—
could he already see them letting go, sinking toward the flowers,
the cows thrashing and roaring, the vigorous goats faltering, the crocodiles feasting
     for now?

Did he wonder what he had gotten into when he began these walks with God?
Did he look into his heart and draw breath to say no?
All or none and the ark this earth that holds us.
Did he ask aloud, What is justice?

I suppose he thought, God is the Lord of Hosts, and I am only Noah—
thinking it was going to be a lot to make an ark in a week, and his wife and his sons

Shem, Ham, and Japheth, and their wives and their children and one pair of every unclean beast and seven pairs of every clean beast was going to be a lot to round up and bring on board.
And I suppose he saw that not even God can keep Himself from choosing

and went home and took his wife in his arms
and later lay in the dark awake and still awake until he got up and howled at the stars.

But l wish he had felt the giants and the great men of his youth at his back and risen to the No.
He could have argued his modest boatbuilding skills, the difficulties in finding and cutting gopher wood.
He could have started on a bigger ark, impossibly huge, multiplying the cubits out to absurdity.
He could have bargained for time, which God has always plenty of.

"America, I Do Not Call Your Name Without Hope"

after Neruda

America, I do not call your name without hope
not even when you lay your knife
against my throat or lace my hands
behind my back, the cuffs connecting
us like two outlaws trying to escape
history's white horse, its heavy whip
a pistolshot in the ear. Lost land,
this is a song for the scars on your back,
for your blistered feet and beautiful
watch, it is for your windmills, your
leavened machines, for your fists. It
is for your wagon of blood, for your dogs
and their teeth of fire, for your sons
and the smoke in their hearts. This is for
your verbs, your long lurk, your whir.
This is for you and your fear, your tar,
for the white heat in your skin and
for your blue bones that one day may sing.
This is for your singing. This is for the past,
but not for what's passed. This is for daybreak
and backbreak, for dreams and for darkness.
This song is not for your fight, but it is a song
for fighting. It is a song of flame, but not for burning.
It is a song out of breath but a plea for breathing.
It is the song I will sing when you knock
on my door, my son's name in your mouth.

Make a Law So That the Spine
Remembers Wings

Incantation

Human reason is beautiful and invincible.
No bars, no barbed wire, no pulping of books,
No sentence of banishment can prevail against it.
It establishes the universal ideas in language,
And guides our hand so we write Truth and Justice
With capital letters, lie and oppression with small.
It puts what should be above things as they are,
Is an enemy of despair and a friend of hope.
It does not know Jew from Greek or slave from master,
Giving us the estate of the world to manage.
It saves austere and transparent phrases
From the filthy discord of tortured words.
It says that everything is new under the sun,
Opens the congealed fist of the past.
Beautiful and very young are Philo-Sophia
And poetry, her ally in the service of the good.
As late as yesterday Nature celebrated their birth,
The news was brought to the mountains by a unicorn and an echo.
Their friendship will be glorious, their time has no limit.
Their enemies have delivered themselves to destruction.

Berkeley, 1968

Translated by the author and Robert Pinsky

The 45th Psalm

Lord, don't let us give over our daughters
and sons, our empire and atoms splitting,
our embryos, arroyos, frontiers, stars
shooting across the sky and manacled
to our amendments. Lord, don't let us give
up hope. Let us call desire a kingdom,
and naïveté the root of all being.
Let us call America matriarch
brawling in the moonlight, gutter blessing,
vast mesa swooning possibility,
violent old umbilical fiction,
wounded badger, rabid fretfully quilled
porcupine, sweet brown muzzle of a stray,
endless orchard of rotten jubilees.
Render equally caliber and psalm.
Quiver us with mercy and forgiveness.
When the powerful arrow us with wreck,
let us aria ourselves unbounded.
Let us sing the rose inside out, eagle
ourselves into hymns, and hymnal ourselves
into clover, prairie, rocket's red glare,
flag triangled from a soldier's casket.
Lord, don't let us anthem ourselves with stripes
and handcuffs, welts and beautiful cages.
Lord, let us pledge allegiance to the meek,
reject the bomb, the bombast, the language
of tirade, tyrant, the compendium
of invective pliéing one nation.
Let us river out, indivisible.
Let us yellow spindrift and chickadee.
Let us aloe on from sea to shining.
Let us pray for a promise unshackled.
Let's have faith in bee zigzagging bramble.
God bless the mule, the plow, the molecules
in my fingertips as I write this line,

the millennia slumbering inside
the small dot at the end of this sentence,
the histories buried in my saying,
the slow painful cottoning to justice.
Let us rewrite our own carnal memoirs
without suspending habeas corpus.
Let us perpetually immigrate,
our visas printed on buffalo hides,
our ID cards etched in the eye socket
of an antelope skull; let us praise You
alike in the bluest sky and in storm cloud.

Gorgon

Now that you need your prescription glasses to see the stars
and now that the telemarketers know your preference in sexual positions

Now that corporations run the government
and move over the land like giant cloud formations

Now that the human family has turned out to be a conspiracy against the planet

Now that it's hard to cast stones
without hitting a cell phone tower
                              that will show up later on your bill

Now that you know you are neither innocent, nor powerful,
nor a character in a book;

You have arrived at the edge of the world
where the information wind howls incessantly

and you stand in your armor made of irony
with your sword of good intentions raised—

The world is a Gorgon.
It holds up its thousand ugly heads
               with their thousand writhing visages

Death or madness to look at it too long

but your job is not to conquer it;

not to provide entertaining repartee,
not to revile yourself in shame.

Your job is to stay calm
Your job is to watch and take notes
To go on looking

Your job is to not be turned into stone.

The Thermometer and the Future

MICHAEL BENEDIKT

This cold is awful, how did the temperature get down there so low? It must have slipped down there by sneaking past us, all hunched over, dressed in the black cloak of night. Because this morning, we are shocked to awake to a white world of magic: all the hailstones bouncing, and our spit suspended. It's time now to make a decision which is truly a matter of life and death: whether to leave right now, in search of some other, more congenial climate; or, if we haven't the nerve to leave, whether to solve everything by becoming a snowman, which is to say the kind of man who only grows when it snows.

Death March, 1945

for Ben-Zion Gold

"There was a muddy ditch at the side of the road
where the road took a sudden turn. If I could jump—."
Five *Muselmänner* abreast, the trekking dead,
skeletons on the march to some other camp.

"I came up with a plan: if it wasn't already too late,
if the weather held, if the guard didn't turn his head,
by the grace of dark I'd make my way to the right
and take my chances. Chances were all I had."

"Where in that hell did you find the nerve to live?
You knew what lay ahead if you were caught."
I thought he'd say, "No choice. Jump or be killed,"

but he wasn't giving lessons on being brave.
"I was loved," he said, "when I was a child."
I tell his story every chance I get.

To the Women Marching, from a Mother at Home

It's cold, and my son is small.
I rock him in the fragile boat of my body
between this night's dark and a brighter shore.

We are always awake.

He curves at my breast like a comma
between the words anchored deep in my chest
and the breath taking form in his lungs.

In the quiet, we hear your chanting.

Remember us with you, we are the rear guard.
I am carrying him like a banner, feel him
cutting his teeth on my curdled milk.

I am sharpening him like an arrow.

Make a Law So That the Spine Remembers Wings

So that the truant boy may go steady with the State,
So that in his spine a memory of wings
Will make his shoulders tense & bend
Like a thing already flown
When the bracelets of another school of love
Are fastened to his wrists,
Make a law that doesn't have to wait
Long until someone comes along to break it.

So that in jail he will have the time to read
How the king was beheaded & the hawk that rode
The king's wrist died of a common cold,
And learn that chivalry persists,
And what first felt like an insult to the flesh
Was the blank "o" of love.
Put the fun back into punishment.
Make a law that loves the one who breaks it.

So that no empty court will make a judge recall
Ice fishing on some overcast bay,
Shivering in the cold beside his father, it ought
To be an interesting law,
The kind of thing that no one can obey,
A law that whispers "Break me."
Let the crows roost & caw.
A good judge is an example to us all.

So that the patrolman can still whistle
"The Yellow Rose of Texas" through his teeth
And even show some faint gesture of respect
While he cuffs the suspect,
Not ungently, & says things like *OK,*
That's it, relax,
It'll go better for you if you don't resist,
Lean back just a little, against me.

The Tradition

Aster. Nasturtium. Delphinium. We thought
Fingers in dirt meant it was our dirt, learning
Names in heat, in elements classical
Philosophers said could change us. *Star Gazer.*
Foxglove. Summer seemed to bloom against the will
Of the sun, which news reports claimed flamed hotter
On this planet than when our dead fathers
Wiped sweat from their necks. *Cosmos. Baby's Breath.*
Men like me and my brothers filmed what we
Planted for proof we existed before
Too late, sped the video to see blossoms
Brought in seconds, colors you expect in poems
Where the world ends, everything cut down.
John Crawford. Eric Garner. Mike Brown.

The Chrysalis

I watched history unfold today.
It happened in a classroom.
There was a girl with a guitar.
There was a girl with a song.
There was a girl with a love she was willing to share.
There was girl with a wooden stool and a voice, both shook slightly.
There was a girl who blew us all away.

I watched history unfold today.
It happened in a classroom.
There was a boy with a book.
There was a boy with a poem.
There was a boy with a love he had found against all odds.
There was a ragged carpet and a pair of hands, both were slightly worn.
There was a boy who blew us all away.

I watched chaos unfold today.
It happened in a heart with a scar.
There was a face faking a smile.
There was a face yelling a word.

But then I was pulled away from the window
By a voice that cried out to be heard.
It said softly that it loved the sound of the rain.
It said strongly that it loved the color of flowers.
It said passionately that it liked grass better than carpet.
It said kindly that it wanted to know what happened.
I didn't catch the beginning but I heard enough to know
that history was being made.

It happened in a word.
That word was any word.
The word was *love*.
The word was *caring*.
The word was a difference because it wasn't shouted.
The word was any change it could make.

In the end the word was *sane*.

Poem for the Future

It was difficult to connect the dots.
We rose and fell while sitting perfectly still.
The wood grain of our desks was so smooth
we thought the tree had figured something out
we hadn't even begun to consider.
We adjusted to what was called *progress*.
Our thumbs took a hook shape from transferring thoughts
to tiny machines which suggested pictures for feelings.
Face circles were a good place to hide what we really felt
from ourselves. But the body didn't lie.
It reflected the choices we made or weren't allowed to make.
It tried to communicate what was happening inside.
Mostly, we were too busy to listen. Some people heard
their footfall while others didn't.
We confused attention for love and so often the attention
was split. Earth suffered the most.
We kept puncturing the biosphere and trying to repair.
It was our envelope.
Some knew about the Echo Flower that grew concave
to reflect the sounds of bats.
Some studied how the forest regrew
and knew it was a message.
Some spoke of fading coral. We needed to need less,
give more. We weren't sure
and wouldn't dare say it aloud, but suspected
some people didn't care.
Love was confused with power and that caused deaths.
We were trying to make a circle.
There was constant exchange.
There was learning and forgetting.
There should have been more mirrors.
No, there should have been more vision.
Sometimes we dove into a lake, glimpsing ourselves just before
we slipped into the water, felt a sudden release of gravity,
and were happy. Happiness—have you felt that?
In such moments, we didn't need to escape ourselves.
There was no place we'd rather be.

America Will Be

after Langston Hughes

I am now at the age where my father calls me brother
when we say goodbye. *Take care of yourself, brother,*
he whispers a half beat before we hang up the phone,
and it is as if some great bridge has unfolded over the air
between us. He is 68 years old. He was born in the throat
of Jim Crow Alabama, one of ten children, their bodies side
by side in the kitchen each morning like a pair of hands
exalting. Over breakfast, I ask him to tell me the hardest thing
about going to school back then, expecting a history
I have already memorized. Boycotts & attack dogs, fire
hoses, Bull Connor in his personal tank, candy paint
shining white as a slaver's ghost. He says: *Having to read
the Canterbury Tales.* He says: *Eating lunch alone.* Now, I hear
the word *America* & think first of my father's loneliness,
the hands holding the pens that stabbed him as he walked
through the hallway, unclenched palms settling
onto a wooden desk, taking notes, trying to pretend
the shame didn't feel like an inheritance. You say *democracy*
& I see the men holding documents that sent him off
to war a year later, Motown blaring from a country
boy's bunker as napalm scarred the sky into jigsaw
patterns, his eyes open wide as the blooming blue
heart of the light bulb in a Crown Heights basement
where he & my mother will dance for the first time, their bodies
swaying like rockets in the impossible dark & yes I know
that this is more than likely not what you mean
when you sing *liberty* but it is the only kind
I know or can readily claim, the times where those hunted
by history are underground & somehow daring to love
what they cannot hold or fully fathom when the stranger
is not a threat but the promise of a different ending.
I woke up this morning & there were men on television
lauding a wall big enough to box out an entire world,
families torn with the stroke of a pen, citizenship

little more than some garment that can be stolen or reduced
to cinder at a tyrant's whim. My father knows this grew up
knowing this witnessed firsthand the firebombs
the Klan multiple messiahs love soaked & shot through
somehow still believes in this grand blood-stained
experiment still votes still prays that his children might
make a life unlike any he has ever seen. He looks
at me like the promise of another cosmos & I never
know what to tell him. All of the books in my head
have made me cynical and distant, but there's a choir
in him that calls me forward, my disbelief built as it is
from the bricks of his belief not in any America
you might see on network news or hear heralded
before a football game but in the quiet
power of Sam Cooke singing that he was born
by a river that remains unnamed that he runs
alongside to this day, some vast & future country
some nation within a nation, black as candor,
loud as the sound of my father's
unfettered laughter over cheese eggs & coffee
his eyes shut tight as armories, his fists
unclenched as if he were invincible.

Allegro

I play Haydn after a black day
and feel a simple warmth in my hands.

The keys are willing. Soft hammers strike.
The resonance green, lively, and calm.

The music says freedom exists
and someone doesn't pay the emperor tax.

I push down my hands in my Haydnpockets
and imitate a person looking on the world calmly.

I hoist the Haydnflag—it signifies:
"We don't give in. But want peace."

The music is a glasshouse on the slope
where the stones fly, the stones roll.

And the stones roll right through
but each pane stays whole.

Translated by Robin Fulton

When They Arrive

When those radiant mango-eyed beings
finally light down on the wheat fields
and ballparks of our planet, it won't be

to speak with our leaders; they won't ask
to be taken to the summit or talk about
trade. They will come for the trees.

They'll ask to be brought to the shade
of banyans and old-growth redwoods.
To the ancient cedars of Lebanon.

They will come to sit with the elders.
To sink their feet into the earth
and drink with them. They will come

for the understory, to listen for the urgencies
that stir up longing and break the seed.
They will hope to practice the art of standing

upright in two worlds—to share secrets
with mushrooms and larvae while
holding a bird in the palm of your hand.

Theirs will not be to puzzle over gravity
or strategies for keeping boots on the ground.
They will come for the other law—

the upward surge, the inexorable craving
for starlight—and dark matter, that melancholy
chord that braids through and through it.

Sunlight Bets on the Come

The basic pleasures remain unchanged,
                                and their minor satisfactions—
Chopping wood, building a fire,
Watching the elk herd
                splinter and cruise around the outcrop of spruce trees

As the deer haul ass,
                their white flags like synchronized swimmers' hands,
Sunlight sealing—stretched like Saran Wrap—
The world as we know it,
                keeping it fresh-flamed should tomorrow arrive.

The Laughter of Women

The laughter of women sets fire
to the Halls of Injustice
and the false evidence burns
to a beautiful white lightness

It rattles the Chambers of Congress
and forces the windows wide open
so the fatuous speeches can fly out

The laughter of women wipes the mist
from the spectacles of the old;
it infects them with a happy flu
and they laugh as if they were young again

Prisoners held in underground cells
imagine that they see daylight
when they remember the laughter of women

It runs across water that divides,
and reconciles two unfriendly shores
like flares that signal the news to each other

What a language it is, the laughter of women,
high-flying and subversive.
Long before law and scripture
we heard the laughter, we understood freedom.

Let Them Not Say

Let them not say: we did not see it.
We saw.

Let them not say: we did not hear it.
We heard.

Let them not say: they did not taste it.
We ate, we trembled.

Let them not say: it was not spoken, not written.
We spoke,
we witnessed with voices and hands.

Let them not say: they did nothing.
We did not-enough.

Let them say, as they must say something:

A kerosene beauty.
It burned.

Let them say we warmed ourselves by it,
read by its light, praised,
and it burned.

January 20, 2017, Academy of American of Poets' Poem-a-Day

Notes on the Poems

Page 8, "SONNET XII: On the Detraction Which Followed Upon My Writing Certain Treatises"
The "treatises" mentioned are the political tracts Milton published in 1643–44 arguing for leniency in divorce laws. For this he was attacked and hauled before the House of Lords. For Latona's twins and the croaking frogs, see Ovid, *Metamorphoses*, Book 6.

Page 9, "Antigone Marches on Washington"
From a high school poetry anthology published by the Marin Poetry Center in 2017. In Sophocles' *Antigone*, Polynices has been killed during the war of the Seven Against Thebes, and to punish him for fighting with the rebels, King Creon orders his body left on the battlefield, unburied. In defiance of the king, Polynices' sister, Antigone, attempts to bury her brother with full sacred rites. The king has Antigone arrested and condemns her to be buried alive in a cave. Haemon, her lover and the king's son, attempts to intervene on her behalf, but to no avail. Antigone kills herself, as does Haemon when he learns of her death.

Page 29, "An Iris for Hillary, January 20, 2017: A Cento"
Centos are poems made by assembling lines from poems by other poets. Here, on Inauguration Day, 2017, a group of women poets are called to testify.

Page 32, "From the Republic of Conscience"
Written at the request of Amnesty International Ireland, to mark International Human Rights Day, 1985. Amnesty International's highest award, the Ambassador of Conscience, was inspired by the poem.

Page 37, "War Voyeurs"
Clara Fraser (1923–98) was a feminist, political organizer, founder of the Freedom Socialist Party, and author of *Revolution, She Wrote*.

Page 63, "Violaceae"
Author's note: "I wrote this poem on a hike the day after the suicide bombing in Manchester. The poem is not a response to the tragedy, though the suffering and potential responses to that suffering were lurking in the back of my mind. This poem is more of an alternative for than a response to. Violaceae is the family name for the group of plants containing the five hundred–plus species of violets."

Page 78, from *The Tempest*, Act I, Scene ii
The Tempest was written in 1610–11, roughly the dawn of the slave trade in the American colonies. The first African slaves were brought to Jamestown, Virginia, in 1619. "Caliban's retort might be taken as self-indictment: even with the gift of language, his nature is so debased that he can only learn to curse. But the lines refuse to mean this; what we experience instead is a sense of their devastating justness. Ugly, rude, savage, Caliban nevertheless achieves for an instant an absolute if intolerably

bitter moral victory" (Stephen Greenblatt, *Learning to Curse: Essays in Early Modern Culture* [New York: Routledge Classics, 2007], 35).

Page 79, from *Voyage of the Sable Venus,* Catalog 4
Robin Coste Lewis's book is a narrative poem about the black female body in art. It is described in the book's prologue as being "comprised solely and entirely of the titles, catalog entries, or exhibit descriptions of Western art objects in which a black female figure is present, dating from 38,000 bce to the present."

Page 80, "America Gives Its Blackness Back to Me"
"Slavery was the monster that made monsters of its masters" (Ta-Nehisi Coates, in "Five Books to Make You Less Stupid About the Civil War," *The Atlantic Magazine,* November 1, 2017).

Page 82, "Jubilee Blues"
One of the Jubilee poems in Tyehimba Jess's *Olio.* The Jubilee poems are imagined in the voices of the Fisk Jubilee Choir, an African-American a capella ensemble begun by students of Fisk University in 1871. Each of the Jubilee poems is "enclosed" on its page by a list of black churches.

Author's note: "The names of our burned and bombed black churches enfold the spirituals sung by our Jubilee choir. Inside each flame burns hum, prayer, and holy book. Each hymn inhabits heat and smolder; each biblical spark is kindled with story."

Page 95, "At Standing Rock"
A rhupunt is a Welsh poetic form of four-syllable lines divided into stanzas and linked by alliteration, internal rhyme, and end rhyme.

Author's note: "The Fort Laramie Treaty of 1851 recognized the sovereignty of the Lakota Sioux over the Great Plains 'as long as the river flows and the eagle flies.' The Fort Laramie Treaty of 1868 prohibited white settlement in the Black Hills for all time, but the subsequent discovery of gold generated an influx of miners who violated the treaty with impunity. [In 2016,] the Lakota protested construction of the Dakota Access Pipeline on the grounds that the project would contaminate their sole source of drinking water and disrupt their sacred lands. The completed pipeline passes under the Missouri River less than one mile upstream of the Standing Rock Reservation."

Page 110, "Blad"
Author's note: "I am the founder and director of Every Campus a Refuge, a program that advocates for temporarily housing refugees on college and university campus grounds and assisting them in resettlement. This poem is based on a conversation I had with the teenage son of the first Syrian refugee family we hosted on our campus. . . . The title is the colloquial Levantine Arabic for *old country* and what folks (those who have left) use nostalgically to refer to their homeland (especially Palestine, Syria and Lebanon). In Modern Standard Arabic, it means *countries.*"

Page 112, "You shall leave behind all you most dearly love"
At the midpoint of *Paradiso*, while traveling through the heavens, Dante the pilgrim meets his great-

great-grandfather, Cacciaguida, who looks into the future and foresees the pilgrim's fate: lifelong political exile from his beloved Florence. This form of exile was the condition in which Dante wrote the *Divine Comedy*, including this passage. Cacciaguida is speaking.

Page 113, "The New Colossus"
Written in 1883 as part of an effort to raise money for the construction of the Statue of Liberty's pedestal. The statue itself was completed in 1886; the poem was engraved and mounted on the pedestal in 1903.

Page 114, "That Damned Fence"
A poem circulated by inmates of the Japanese-American Internment Camp, Poston, Arizona, 1942–45. Poston was the largest of ten American concentration camps run by the War Relocation Authority during World War II.

Page 132, "Kara Walker's Sphinx"
Kara Walker's sculpture, *A Subtlety*, or *The Marvelous Sugar Baby*, is subtitled *An Homage to the unpaid and overworked Artisans who have refined our Sweet tastes from the cane fields to the Kitchens of the New World on the Occasion of the demolition of the Domino Sugar Refining Plant*. A public art work, it is approximately 75 1/2 feet long, and 34 1/2 feet high, and made of white sugar rather than unbleached brown sugar. The title of Walker's sculpture comes from her reading of *Sweetness and Power: The Place of Sugar in Modern History*, where she learned that "in the eleventh century, marzipan sculptures were created by the sultans in the East to give to the poor on feast days. This tradition made its way to Northern Europe, eventually, where royal chefs made sugar sculptures called subtleties. Walker was taken not only with those stories but with the history of the slave trade in America: Who cut the sugar cane? Who ground it down to syrup? Who bleached it? Who sacked it?" (Hilton Als, "The Sugar Sphinx," *The New Yorker*, May 8, 2014).

Page 150, "England in 1819"
This poem by Shelley, who elsewhere famously referred to poets as "the unacknowledged legislators of the world," was written in response to the so-called Peterloo Massacre of 1819 in Manchester, England. A crowd of some sixty thousand had gathered to protest a government unresponsive to economic inequalities. Fearing disorder, and thinking perhaps of the French Revolution, the local police called in the cavalry, who charged the crowd, killing fifteen and injuring many hundreds. No publisher dared publish this poem in 1819, though it circulated by word of mouth. It did not appear in print until 1839, when Mary Shelley published it.

Page 166, "The Chrysalis"
Author's note: "I wrote this poem in Mr. [Eliot] Schain's class, about the auditions we were holding for our fall poetry and art show. . . . It was very shortly after the 2016 election, and there was a student protest going on at the same time. You could hear the protest clearly from Mr. Schain's classroom. . . . It was very loud and angry and afraid. The students in the classroom were no less emotionally affected than those outside, but they had come to that room to express the best parts of themselves in the hopes that it would be a positive influence on the world around them."

Page 168, "America Will Be"

This poem refers to (and draws its title from) the penultimate stanza of the Langston Hughes poem "Let America Be America Again," also quoted in an epigraph of this book. The Hughes poem was written in 1935 and originally published in *Esquire* in 1936.

Contributors' Notes

DIYA ABDO is associate professor of English at Guilford College, NC. She has published poetry, fiction, and creative nonfiction and is the founding director of *Every Campus a Refuge,* which houses refugees on campus grounds and assists them in resettlement.

ELLERY AKERS is the author of two poetry books, *Practicing the Truth* and *Knocking on the Earth.* She has won the Poetry International Prize, the John Masefield Award, and *Sierra* magazine's Nature Writing Award, among others. Her poetry has been featured on National Public Radio and in *The New York Times Magazine, Poetry,* and *The Sun.*

JOSE A. ALCANTARA's poems have appeared in *The Southern Review, Rattle, The American Journal of Poetry, Beloit Poetry Journal, The Midwest Quarterly,* and *Spoon River Poetry Review,* among other journals. A former Fishtrap Fellow, he was awarded the 2017 Patricia Bibby Memorial Scholarship from Tebot Bach. He works as a bookstore clerk in Aspen, Colorado.

ELIZABETH ALEXANDER is the author of six books of poetry, including *American Sublime, Antebellum Dream Book,* and most recently, *Crave Radiance.* She has taught at Yale, where she chaired the African American Studies department, and Columbia University. In 2009, she read her poem "Praise Song for the Day" at the presidential inauguration ceremony for Barack Obama.

DANTE ALIGHIERI (c. 1265–1321) wrote the most important poem of the Middle Ages, the *Divine Comedy.* Written in the vernacular, rather than Latin as was most poetry at that time, his three-part work (Hell, Purgatory, and Heaven) is considered the greatest poem in the Italian language and paved the way for Petrarch and Boccaccio. He is known in Italy simply as *il Poeta.*

RICK BAROT has published three books of poetry: *Chord,* which received the 2016 UNT Prize, the PEN Open Book Award, and the Thom Gunn Award; *Want,* which won the 2009 Grub Street Book Prize; and *The Darker Fall,* which received the Kathryn A. Morton Book Prize. Barot is the poetry editor for *The New England Review.* His fourth book of poems, *The Galleons,* is forthcoming in 2020.

ELLEN BASS has written three books of poetry: *Like a Beggar, The Human Line,* and *Mules of Love,* which won The Lambda Literary Award. She coedited *No More Masks,* the first major anthology of women's poetry. She has received fellowships from the NEA and the California Arts Council, among other honors. Bass is a chancellor of the Academy of American Poets.

DAVID BECKMAN's chapbooks include *Language Factory of the Mind* (Finishing Line Press) and *Phantasia* (mgv2/publishing, France). His work has appeared in *Spillway 18* and *20*; two Marin Poetry Center anthologies; *Ambush Review 3, 4,* and *5*; and *x-peri,* among others.

BEI DAO was a member of the Misty Poets group, who wrote in resistance to the Cultural Revolution in China. He is known for his pro-democracy poem "The Answer," written during the Tiananmen Square demonstrations in 1976. Exiled from China from 1989 to 2006, he lives, teaches, and continues to publish in Europe. He has been nominated for the Nobel Prize in Literature numerous times.

DAN BELLM is the author of four books of poetry, most recently *Deep Well.* His other books are *Practice,* named one of the Top Ten Poetry Books of 2008 by *The Virginia Quarterly Review; Buried Treasure; One Hand on the Wheel;* and *Terrain* (with Molly Fisk and Forrest Hamer). His honors include grants from the NEA and the California Arts Council.

MICHAEL BENEDIKT (1935–2007), the poetry editor for *The Paris Review* from 1975 to 1978, was also the editor of two important twentieth-century poetry anthologies: *The Poetry of Surrealism* (1974) and *The Prose Poem* (1976). He was a literary critic and the author of five books of poetry, including *Night Cries* and *The Badminton at Great Barrington*.

JOSHUA BENNETT hails from Yonkers, New York. He is the author of *The Sobbing School* (Penguin, 2016) and the forthcoming *Being Property Once Myself: Blackness and the End of Man* (Harvard University Press, 2019) and *Owed* (Penguin, 2020). A junior fellow in the Society of Fellows at Harvard University, Bennett is an assistant professor of English and Creative Writing at Dartmouth College.

REGINALD DWAYNE BETTS is the author of two books of poetry, *Shahid Reads His Own Palm* and *Bastards of the Reagan Era*. His memoir, *A Question of Freedom*, won the 2010 NAACP Image Award. He graduated from the MFA program at Warren Wilson College, earned a JD from Yale Law School, and is currently enrolled in the PhD in Law program at Yale.

FRANK BIDART was awarded the 2018 Pulitzer Prize for Poetry and the 2017 National Book Award for Poetry for his book *Half-Light: Collected Poems 1965–2016*. His other collections of poetry include *Metaphysical Dog* (2013), which won the National Book Critics Circle Award. He was the 2007 winner of Yale University's Bollingen Prize in American Poetry.

WILLIAM BLAKE (1757–1827), an English poet, painter, and printmaker, is considered one of the major figures of the Romantic movement. A mystic and visionary, he created a series of "prophetic works" that saw the imagination as an emanation of divinity. His most famous poetical works are *Songs of Innocence and Experience* and *The Marriage of Heaven and Hell*.

CHANA BLOCH (1940–2017) was the author of six books of poetry, including *Mrs. Dumpty*, *Blood Honey*, and *Swimming in the Rain*. A posthumous collection, *The Moon Is Almost Full*, was published in 2017. She co-translated the biblical *Song of Songs*, *The Selected Poetry of Yehuda Amichai*, and Amichai's *Open Closed Open*, which won the 2001 PEN Award for Poetry in Translation.

HEATHER BOURBEAU wrote the poetry collection *Daily Palm Castings*, was nominated for a Pushcart Prize, and has worked for the UN peacekeeping mission in Liberia and UNICEF Somalia. Her journalism has appeared in *The Economist*, *The Financial Times*, and *Foreign Affairs*.

JERICHO BROWN's first collection of poetry, *Please*, won the 2009 American Book Award. His second, *The New Testament*, received the Anisfield-Wolf Book Award in 2015. He has received a Whiting Writer's Award as well as fellowships from the NEA, the Radcliffe Institute at Harvard University, and the Guggenheim Foundation.

JOCELYN CASEY-WHITEMAN is author of the chapbook *Lure*. Her poems have appeared in *Boston Review*, *DIAGRAM*, *jubilat*, *Sixth Finch*, *Verse Daily*, and elsewhere. She teaches creative writing and yoga in New York City.

C. P. CAVAFY (1863–1933), an Egyptian Greek poet, lived most of his adult life in Alexandria. His major works, mostly written after his fortieth birthday, were not published until two years after his death. Gradual recognition of his work has made him one of the most honored Greek poets of modern times. He is best known for his poems "Waiting for the Barbarians" and "Ithaca."

THOMAS CENTOLELLA is the author of four collections of poetry, the most recent being *Almost Human*, winner of the Dorset Prize from Tupelo Press. His honors include the Lannan Literary Award and the American Book Award.

LUCILLE CLIFTON (1936–2010) was the author of fourteen collections of poetry, including *Two-Headed Woman*, which won the Juniper Prize. She is known for her many poems celebrating the black body, among them "homage to my hips." She was the recipient of many prestigious awards, including the posthumous Robert Frost Medal for lifetime achievement from the Poetry Society of America.

Susan Cohen has published a nonfiction book, two poetry chapbooks, and two full-length poetry collections: *Throat Singing* (WordTech, 2012) and *A Different Wakeful Animal* (Meadowhawk Prize, Red Dragonfly Press, 2016.) A former journalist, she earned an MFA from Pacific University.

Laura Da', a member of the Eastern Shawnee tribe of Oklahoma, is the author of two books of poetry: a chapbook, *The Tecumseh Motel*, published in *Effigies II*, and a full-length collection, *Tributaries* (University of Arizona, 2015). She received a Native Arts and Cultures Foundation Fellowship in 2015.

Matt Daly is a poet, visual artist, and teacher from Jackson, Wyoming. His writing has been published in various journals and anthologies. He is a resident faculty member of the Jackson Hole Writers Conference. More information is available at www.dalypoetry.com.

Patrick Daly's poem "Words" was a 2015 poem-of-the-year in the *New Statesman*. His poem "Tiananmen Square" received honorable mention in the Pushcart Prizes, and his chapbook "Playing with Fire" won the Abby Niebauer Memorial Prize.

Mahmoud Darwish (1941–2008), a Palestinian poet, published over thirty books of poetry during his lifetime. Considered a symbol of Palestinian resistance to Israel, he also hoped for reconciliation between the two countries. The poet Naomi Shihab Nye has written that Darwish "is the essential breath of the Palestinian people, the eloquent witness of exile and belonging. . . ."

Lucille Lang Day has published ten poetry collections and chapbooks, including *Becoming an Ancestor* and *Dreaming of Sunflowers: Museum Poems*. She has also authored two children's books, *Chain Letter* and *The Rainbow Zoo*, and a memoir, *Married at Fourteen*.

Mai Der Vang's poetry collection *Afterland* won the 2016 Walt Whitman Award from the Academy of American Poets. A co-editor of *How Do I Begin: A Hmong American Literary Anthology*, she is a visiting writer at the School of the Art Institute of Chicago, a Kundiman Fellow, and the recipient of a Lannan Literary Fellowship.

Ann DeVilbiss has had work published in *CALYX, Crab Orchard Review, Day One*, and elsewhere. She is the recipient of an Emerging Artist Award from the Kentucky Arts Council, which is supported by state tax dollars and federal funding from the National Endowment for the Arts. You can find more of her work at anndevilbiss.com.

Natalie Diaz, a Mojave American poet, is enrolled in the Gila River Indian Community. Her first poetry collection, *When My Brother Was an Aztec*, was a 2012 Lannan Literary Selection. She is a member of the faculty at Arizona State University.

Emily Dickinson published very little during her lifetime, but her intense, brief lyric poems were eventually made available to the public, first in altered versions and finally in authentic ones, establishing her as a unique voice and the most important woman poet in American letters.

Carol Dine's book of poems, *Orange Night*, is accompanied with images by acclaimed artist and Holocaust survivor Samuel Bak. *Van Gogh in Poems* narrates Vincent's creative process. Her manuscript, "Resistance: The Canvas of War," brings forth the voices of global women. For this work, she received a grant from the Money for Women/Barbara Deming Memorial Fund.

Dante Di Stefano is the author of *Love Is a Stone Endlessly in Flight* (Brighthorse Books, 2016). He is the co-editor, with Maria Isabel Alvarez, of the anthology *Misrepresented People: Poetic Responses to Trump's America* (NYQ Books, 2017).

183

SUSAN G. DUNCAN is an independent consultant with a performing and visual arts clientele. She served as executive director for San Francisco's long-running musical comedy phenomenon *Beach Blanket Babylon*, the California Shakespeare Theater, and the Grammy-winning all-male vocal ensemble Chanticleer. Her poetry has appeared in *Atlanta Review*, *The MacGuffin*, and *Thema*, among others.

CAMILLE T. DUNGY has written four books of poetry: *What to Eat, What to Drink, What to Leave for Poison*; *Suck on the Marrow*; *Smith Blue*; and most recently, *Trophic Cascade* (2017). Her collection of personal essays, *Guidebook to Relative Strangers,* was nominated for a Book Critics Circle Award in 2018. Her honors include an American Book Award and two Northern California Book Awards.

CHIYUMA ELLIOTT is an assistant professor of African American Studies at the University of California, Berkeley. She is the author of two books: *California Winter League* (2015) and *Vigil* (2017).

MOLLY FISK, a poet and radio commentator, is the author, most recently, of *Houston, We Have a Possum* and *The More Difficult Beauty*. She's the inaugural poet laureate of Nevada County, California, and an NEA fellow.

JEN STEWART FUESTON lives in Longmont, Colorado. Her work has appeared in a wide variety of journals and anthologies. Her forthcoming poem "Trying to Conceive" was a finalist for *Ruminate* magazine's McCabe poetry prize. Her chapbook, *Visitations*, was published in 2015 by Finishing Line Press. She has taught writing at the University of Colorado Boulder and abroad.

MOLLY GILES is the author of a novel, *Iron Shoes*, and four award-winning collections of short stories, including *Creek Walk and Other Stories* and *Rough Translations*, which won the Flannery O'Connor Award for Short Fiction.

MIRIAM BIRD GREENBERG's book *In the Volcano's Mouth* won the 2015 Agnes Lynch Starrett Prize from the University of Pittsburgh Press. She is also the author of two chapbooks, *all night in the new country* (Sixteen Rivers Press) and *Pact-Blood, Fevergrass* (Ricochet Editions). Her honors include fellowships from the NEA, the Provincetown Fine Arts Work Center, and the Poetry Foundation.

SUSAN GRIFFIN, a feminist poet and essayist with an abiding focus on ecology and nature, has written more than twenty books, among them *Unremembered Country: Poems* and *Bending Home: Selected New Poems*. Her landmark books of essays include *Woman and Nature: The Roaring Inside Her* and *Wrestling with the Angel of Democracy: On Being an American Citizen* (2008).

JUDY HALEBSKY is the author of the poetry collections *Sky=Empty* and *Tree Line,* and the chapbook *Space/Gap/Interval/Distance*. Originally from Halifax, Nova Scotia, she now lives in Oakland and teaches at Dominican University of California.

FORREST HAMER is the author of *Call and Response* (Alice James, 1995), winner of the Beatrice Hawley Award; *Middle Ear* (Roundhouse, 2000), winner of the Northern California Book Award; and *Rift* (Four Way Books, 2007). He is also a psychoanalyst.

ROBERT HASS is the author or editor of numerous books of poems, essays, and translations, most recently *A Little Book on Form: An Exploration into the Formal Imagination of Poetry*. Hass served as poet laureate of the United States from 1995 to 1997, and in 2007, his book of poems *Time and Material* won the 2007 National Book Award and the Pulitzer Prize.

ROBERT HAYDEN (1913–80) was celebrated for his poetic craftsmanship and his writings about black life and the Vietnam War, though he sometimes resisted being labeled a black poet. His most anthologized poem is "Those Winter Sundays," a poem about his father. Hayden served as a consultant in poetry to the Library of Congress from 1976 to 1978, a position later known as poet laureate of the United States.

TERRANCE HAYES is the author of *Muscular Music* (1999), which won a Kate Tufts Discovery Award; *Hip Logic* (2002); *Wind in a Box* (2006); *Lighthead* (2010), which won the National Book Award, and most recently, *American Sonnets for My Past and Future Assassin* (2018). All of the seventy poems in this book were written during the first two hundred days of the Trump administration. His many honors include a MacArthur Foundation award and a Guggenheim.

SEAMUS HEANEY (1929–2013), considered one of the greatest poets of the twentieth century, grew up in Northern Ireland. He was the author of twelve books of poetry and four selected editions of his work, much of which dealt with his family, local life, Irish history, and the Troubles that roiled his country during his lifetime. In 1995, he was awarded the Nobel Prize in Literature.

JUAN FELIPE HERRERA, whose parents were migrant workers, served as the poet laureate of the United States from 2015 to 2017. The author of many books of poetry, prose, young adult novels, and children's books, he received the 2008 National Book Critics Circle Award in Poetry for *Half the World in Light.*

BRENDA HILLMAN is the author of ten books of poetry, including *Practical Water*, for which she won the LA Times Book Award for Poetry, and *Seasonal Works with Letters on Fire*, which received the 2014 Griffin Poetry Prize and the Northern California Book Award for Poetry. Her most recent book, *Extra Hidden Life among the Days,* was published in 2018.

JANE HIRSHFIELD has written eight books of poetry, among them *Given Sugar, Given Salt*; *After*; and most recently, *The Beauty* (2017). Her books of essays are *Nine Gates: Entering the Mind of Poetry* and *Ten Windows: How Great Poems Transform the World*. She has edited several collections of poetry and is a chancellor of the Academy of American Poets.

TONY HOAGLAND's book of poetry *What Narcissism Means to Me* was a finalist for the National Book Critics Circle Award. He is the author of five other full-length collections, including his most recent, *Priest Turned Therapist Treats Fear of God* (2018). His honors include two grants from the NEA and a Guggenheim Fellowship.

ROBINSON JEFFERS (1887–1962) lived in Carmel, California, and wrote about nature and human conflict on the central California coast. An early writer of what is known today as "eco-poetry," he became controversial for his opposition to US participation in World War II. His best-known works include "Hurt Hawks," "The Purse-Seine," and "Shine, Perishing Republic."

JANET JENNINGS's work has appeared in *Agni online, Nimrod, Spillway, TriQuarterly*, and *Verse Daily*, among others. She lives in San Anselmo, California, with her husband and twin daughters and is the author of *Traces in Water*, a poetry chapbook.

TYEHIMBA JESS is the author of two books of poetry, *Leadbelly* (2005), which was a winner of the 2004 National Poetry Series competition, and *Olio* (2016), which received the 2017 Pulitzer Prize for Poetry. *Olio* has been described as a collage of sonnets, songs, and narratives about unheralded African American artists, writers, and musicians of the Reconstruction Era.

JAAN KAPLINSKI is an Estonian poet, essayist, and translator. Three of his books have been translated into English, the most recent being *Evening Brings Everything Back*. His work, influenced by Buddhism, focuses on global issues. He has been said to be a contender for the Nobel Prize in Literature.

YUSEF KOMUNYAKAA has published many books of poetry, including *Neon Vernacular*, which received the 1994 Kingsley Tufts Poetry Award and the 1994 Pulitzer Prize for Poetry. His work deals with early black life in the rural South and his military service during the Vietnam War. His most recent

185

book of poetry is *The Emperor of Water Clocks* (2015), and his honors include the Ruth Lilly Poetry Prize.

DANA KOSTER is the author of *Binary Stars* (Carolina Wren Press, 2017). She is a former Stegner Fellow, and her poems have appeared in *EPOCH, Indiana Review, The Collagist*, and many others. She lives in Modesto, California, with her husband and two sons.

SUSANNA LANG's third collection of poems is *Travel Notes from the River Styx* (Terrapin Books, 2017). Her poems have appeared in such journals as *Little Star, Prairie Schooner*, and *december*. She teaches in the Chicago public schools.

EMMA LAZARUS (1849–87), a classically taught poet, translator, and activist, is most famously known as the author of the inscription on the Statue of Liberty. Taken from her sonnet "The New Colossus," these lines have helped to define our country. In the spirit of her poem, Lazarus was instrumental in helping to settle Eastern European Jewish immigrants in the United States.

URSULA K. LE GUIN (1929–2018) is primarily known for her novels written in the genres of fantasy and science fiction, but she was also a poet and essayist who mentored many young writers. In 2014, she was awarded the National Book Foundation Medal for Distinguished Contribution to American Letters. Her last book of poetry was *Late in the Day* (2015).

JULIA B. LEVINE received the 2015 Northern California Book Award in Poetry for her latest collection, *Small Disasters Seen in Sunlight* (LSU Press, 2014); the 2003 Tampa Review Prize for her collection *Ask*; and the 1998 Anhinga Poetry Prize for her first collection, *Practicing for Heaven*. Her other honors include a Neruda Award from *Nimrod* and a Discovery/The Nation award.

PHILIP LEVINE (1928–2015), the author of more than twenty collections of poetry and editions of his works, is especially known for his poems about his Jewish heritage and working life in the factories of Detroit. Levine served as poet laureate of the United States from 2011 to 2012. His posthumous book of poetry, *The Last Shift*, was published in 2018.

LARRY LEVIS (1946–96) grew up in the Central Valley of California and studied under Philip Levine. He published five books during his lifetime, including *The Afterlife*, winner of the Lamont Prize from the Academy of American Poets. Three more books were published posthumously, edited by his colleagues: *Elegy, The Selected Levis*, and *The Darkening Trapeze: Last Poems*.

ROBIN COSTE LEWIS's first collection of poems, *Voyage of the Sable Venus*, won the National Book Award for Poetry. She is the coauthor (with Kevin Young) of the poems in a book of drawings by Robert Rauschenberg, *Thirty-Four Illustrations for Dante's Inferno* (MoMA). Her second book of poetry, *Prosthetic*, is forthcoming from Knopf. Lewis is the poet laureate of Los Angeles.

ADA LIMÓN is the author of five books of poetry, including *Bright Dead Things*, which was a finalist for the National Book Award in Poetry, the Kingsley Tufts Poetry Award, and the National Book Critics Circle Award, and was named one of the Top Ten Poetry Books of the Year by *The New York Times*. Her most recent collection is *The Carrying* (2018).

AUDRE LORDE (1934–92) was a poet, feminist, and civil rights activist. She wrote eight books of poetry, among them *From a Land Where Other People Live*, which was nominated for the National Book Award in 1973, and *Coal*, which made her an important figure in the Black Arts Movement. Her work often explores her black lesbian identity and her anger at social injustice.

ALISON LUTERMAN is a poet, essayist, and playwright. Her books of poetry are *Desire Zoo, The Largest Possible Life*, and *See How We Almost Fly*. She has published in *The Sun, Rattle*, and *Poetry 180,* among many other journals and anthologies, and has taught at the Writing Salon in Berkeley, the Esalen Institute, and the Omega Institute, as well as at high schools, juvenile halls, and poetry festivals.

WILLIAM MATTHEWS (1942–97) was the author of eleven books of poetry, among them *Time & Money*, which won the National Book Critics Circle Award in 1996. In 1997, he received the Ruth Lilly Poetry Prize. His two posthumous collections are *Search Party: Collected Poems* and *After All: Last Poems*. Matthews often wrote about basketball and jazz, among many other subjects.

SHANE MCCRAE is the author of the poetry collections *Mule, Blood, Forgiveness Forgiveness, The Animal Too Big to Kill*, and most recently, *In the Language of My Captor*, a finalist for the 2017 National Book Award and a winner of the 2018 Anisfield-Wolf Book Awards. He is a recipient of the Whiting Award.

DAWN MCGUIRE, a neurologist, is the author of three poetry collections, including *The Aphasia Café*, which won the Indie Book Award for Poetry in 2013. Her poems have appeared in the *Journal of the American Medical Association (JAMA)* and the *Journal of American Neurology*, among others. She is the adjunct professor of neurology at the Neurosciences Institute of Morehouse School of Medicine.

GRACE MCNALLY, a high school senior, was a finalist in the 2015 Marin Young Playwrights' Festival. Her work is featured in the Marin School of the Arts creative writing and visual arts anthology *Coffee Stains and Growing Pains* and the 2017 Marin high school poetry anthology *There Are Greater Songs Than Love Songs*. Her hobbies include fencing, theater, piano, and dancing around her trailer.

JANE MEAD is the author of five collections of poetry, most recently *World of Made and Unmade* (Alice James, 2016). She publishes widely in journals and anthologies and is the recipient of a Guggenheim Foundation Fellowship, a Whiting Writers Award, and a Lannan Foundation Completion Grant. She manages her family's ranch in Northern California and often teaches as a visiting writer.

W. S. MERWIN, poet, writer, translator, and ardent environmentalist, has published many acclaimed collections of poetry over a seventy-year career, including *The Lice*; *The Carrier of Ladders*, which won the Pulitzer Prize for poetry in 1971; *The Vixen*; and *The Shadow of Sirius*, which won the Pulitzer Prize for poetry in 2009. His most recent books of poetry are *Garden Time* and *The Moon Before Morning*.

CZESLAW MILOSZ (1911–2004), one of the greatest poets of the twentieth century, was born in Lithuania to Polish parents. A member of the Polish Resistance in World War II, he defected to France when the Communists came to power. In 1980, he was awarded the Nobel Prize for Literature. His many books of poetry include *Unattainable Earth, Bells in Winter, The Separate Notebooks*, and *Provinces*.

JACK MILLSON is an eighteen-year-old former student at Alhambra High School in Martinez, the last in a long list of towns he has inhabited. The peculiar energy of the Bay Area first captivated him at the age of ten; it has yet to stop. He is published or forthcoming in *Backroads* and *Apprehension* magazines.

JOHN MILTON (1608–74), famed author of the epic poem *Paradise Lost*, was a civil servant for the English Commonwealth and also served under Oliver Cromwell. Writing at a time of religious and political conflict, he was celebrated for his *Areopagitica* (1644), a defense of free speech and freedom of the press. He is considered among the greatest of English poets.

LISEL MUELLER was forced to flee Nazi Germany with her family at the age of fifteen. She has published thirteen books of poetry, including *The Private Life*, the 1975 Lamont Poetry Selection; *The Need to Hold Still* (1980), which received the National Book Award; and *Alive Together: New & Selected Poems* (1996), which won the Pulitzer Prize. Her other awards include the Ruth Lilly Prize.

MERYL NATCHEZ's translations include *Poems from the Stray Dog Café: Akhmatova, Mandelstam and Gumilev* and *Tadeusz Borowski: Selected Poems*. Her poetry collection, *Jade Suit*, appeared in 2001. She is on the board of Marin Poetry Center and blogs at www.dactyls-and-drakes.com.

LEONARD NATHAN (1924–2007) was a poet, critic, translator, and long-time professor of rhetoric at UC Berkeley. He wrote seventeen books of poetry, including *Returning Your Call*, which was nominated for a National Book Award. A mentor of Ted Kooser, among others, his last two books were *Restarting the World* (2006) and *Ragged Sonnets*, which was published posthumously in 2008.

PABLO NERUDA (1904–73) was a poet, politician, and diplomat. Forced to escape Chile in 1948 when communism was outlawed, and possibly murdered by the Pinochet regime following his return, he is considered the national poet of that country. He won the Nobel Prize for Literature in 1971. His many books of poetry include *Twenty Love Poems and a Song of Despair, The Heights of Macchu Picchu, Canto General,* and *Extravagaria*.

GAIL NEWMAN's poems have appeared in journals and anthologies including *Canary, Prairie Schooner, Calyx, Ghosts of the Holocaust, Prism,* and *The Doll Collection*. Her collection of poetry, *One World*, was published by Moon Tide Press. Newman lives in San Francisco, where she works as a poet-teacher for California Poets in the Schools.

NAOMI SHIHAB NYE, the daughter of a Palestinian father and a German-and-Swiss American mother, reflects both cultures in her work. A noted poet of the Southwest, she is also a voice for Arab Americans. Her books include *Hugging the Jukebox, Red Suitcase, Fuel, Transfer,* and *What Have You Lost?* She has received Lannan, Guggenheim, and Witter Bynner fellowships, as well as the Lavan Award.

SHARON OLDS is the author of twelve books of poetry, including *The Dead and the Living*, which was the Lamont Poetry Selection for 1983 and the winner of the National Book Critics Circle Award. Among her other books are *The Gold Cell; One Secret Thing; Stag's Leap*, which won the Pulitzer Prize in 2013; and most recently, *Odes* (2016).

MARTIN OTT's most recent book is *Spectrum* (C&R Press, 2016). The author of seven books, he won the De Novo and Sandeen prizes for his first two poetry collections. His work has appeared in more than two hundred magazines.

GEORGE PERREAULT has served as a visiting writer in New Mexico, Montana, and Utah. His poems have been nominated three times for the Pushcart Prize and selected for fourteen anthologies and dozens of journals.

IRMA PINEDA, a poet, essayist, and translator, is the author of several books of bilingual poetry (Zapotec-Spanish). Her poetry and essays have been translated into many languages and have appeared in various anthologies in America and Europe.

PO CHÜ-I (772–846), a Tang Dynasty Chinese poet, was also a civil servant whose career was marked by both successes and failures, including periods of exile. His poetry, which was influential in Japan, is noted for its clarity and its attention to both social conflict and everyday life. He ended his life as a hermit, during which time he completed his collected works.

TANIA PRYPUTNIEWICZ, author of *November Butterfly* (Saddle Road Press, 2014), is a graduate of the Iowa Writers' Workshop. Her poems recently appeared or are forthcoming in *Chiron Review, Journal of Applied Poetics, Nimrod International Journal, Prime Number Magazine, Silver Birch Press,* and *Whale Road Review*. She teaches a monthly poetry workshop at San Diego Writers, Ink.

DEAN RADER's first book, *Works & Days*, won the 2010 T. S. Eliot Poetry Prize. His second, *Self-Portrait as Wikipedia Entry* (2017), received the Poetry Society of America's George Bogin Award.

Suture, a collection of collaborative poems written with Simone Muench, was also published in 2017, as was the anthology *Bullets into Bells: Poets and Citizens Respond to Gun Violence*, which he coedited.

CLAUDIA RANKINE is the author of five books of poetry, including her first, *Nothing in Nature Is Private*, for which she received the Cleveland State Poetry Prize, and *Citizen: An American Lyric*, which received the 2014 National Book Critics Circle Award in Poetry. Among her numerous awards are a grant from the Lannan Foundation, the Jackson Poetry Prize, and a MacArthur "genius" grant.

LIAM RECTOR (1949–2007) was the author of *The Sorrow of Architecture*, *American Prodigal*, and *The Executive Director of the Fallen World*. He coedited *On the Poetry of Frank Bidart: Fastening the Voice to the Page* and edited *The Day I Was Older: On the Poetry of Donald Hall*. He taught at Columbia University and founded and directed the graduate writing seminars at Bennington College.

ADRIENNE RICH (1929–2012), poet, feminist thinker, and activist in progressive causes, wrote and published two dozen volumes of poetry, including *Diving into the Wreck*, *The Dream of a Common Language*, *A Wild Patience Has Taken Me This Far*, *An Atlas of the Difficult World*, *The School Among the Ruins*, and *Telephone Ringing in the Labyrinth*.

CHRISTOPHER RUBIO-GOLDSMITH was born in Mérida, Yucatán. He grew up and still lives in Tucson, Arizona. After teaching high school English for twenty-seven years, he fills his days with bicycle rides, writing workshops, volunteering, and cooking dinner for Kelly.

MARTIN RUSSELL, who was born, raised, and educated in England. lives in Mill Valley, California. He is a playwright whose work has been produced at the Actors Theatre of Louisville, Kennedy Center, Off Off Broadway, and the Squaw Valley Community of Writers, among others.

KAY RYAN, known for her original voice and subtle wit, has published eight books of poetry, among them *Say Uncle*, *The Niagara River*, *Flamingo Watching*, and *The Best of It: New and Selected Poems* (2010), which won the Pulitzer Prize for Poetry. She received the Ruth Lilly Poetry Prize in 2004 and was the poet laureate of the United States from 2008 to 2010.

TOMAŽ ŠALAMUN (1941–2014), a neo-avant-garde Slovenian poet, was internationally acclaimed as an absurdist. Several of his many books of poetry have been translated into English, including *The Selected Poems of Tomaž Šalamun*; *The Four Questions of Melancholy*; and his last book, *On the Tracks of Wild Game* (2012). He was influenced by Rumi, Frank O'Hara, John Ashbery, and Walt Whitman.

ELIOT SCHAIN's poetry has appeared in *Ploughshares* and *American Poetry Review* and was included in *The Place That Inhabits Us: Poems of the San Francisco Bay Watershed* and *Bear Flag Republic: Prose Poems and Poetics from California*. He lives in Berkeley, California.

PETER DALE SCOTT, an emeritus professor of English, a former diplomat, and a writer of numerous political books, has written eleven books of poetry, including the trilogy *Coming to Jakarta*, *Listening to the Candle*, and *Minding the Darkness*, each a book-length poem. His poetry, like his prose, is concerned with what he terms "deep politics."

PRARTHO SERENO, a former poet laureate of Marin County, California (2015–17), is the author of *Elephant Raga*, *Call from Paris*, and *Causing a Stir: The Secret Lives & Loves of Kitchen Utensils*. She teaches at the College of Marin and is a poet-teacher with California Poets in the Schools.

MONA NICOLE SFEIR was born in New York City and grew up in five states and four countries. She has an MFA from California College of the Arts in San Francisco and is a poet and a visual artist. She currently resides in Washington, DC.

WILLIAM SHAKESPEARE (1564–1616), English poet, playwright, and actor, is considered the greatest writer in the English language. The author of almost forty undying plays, he is also revered for his

154 sonnets and two long narrative poems. His unmatched command of the English language and understanding of the human drama allow the characters in his plays and the subjects of his poems to come alive on the stage and on the page.

SOLMAZ SHARIF is an Iranian-American poet whose first collection of poems, *Look*, won the 2017 American Book Award. A Stegner fellow, her many other honors include the 2014 Ruth Lilly and Dorothy Sargeant Rosenberg Poetry Fellowship, an NEA grant, and the 2017 PEN Center Literary Award for Poetry. She is currently a lecturer at Stanford University.

PERCY BYSSHE SHELLEY (1792–1822), a major Romantic poet, was a member of the aristocracy whose advocacy of atheism, socialism, and free love made him a scandalous figure in his time. His most famous poems include "Ozymandias," "Ode to the West Wind," "To a Skylark," "Music, When Soft Voices Die," and "Adonaïs," his elegy for John Keats.

EVIE SHOCKLEY is the author of five books of poetry, including *half-red sea*; *31 words: prose poems*; *the new black*, for which she received the Hurston/Wright Legacy Award in Poetry; and her most recent, *semiautomatic* (2017). She is a MacDowell Colony Fellow and teaches at Rutgers University–New Brunswick.

AUSTIN SMITH, a Stegner fellow, has published three poetry chapbooks and one full-length collection, *Almanac*, which was chosen by Paul Muldoon for the Princeton Series of Contemporary Poets. Smith's next book, *Flyover Country*, is forthcoming from Princeton. He is currently a lecturer at Stanford University, where he teaches courses in poetry, fiction, environmental literature, and journalism.

DANEZ SMITH is the author of *[insert] boy*, winner of the Kate Tufts Discovery Award and the Lambda Literary Award for Gay Poetry. His most recent book is *Don't Call Us Dead* (2017), a finalist for the National Book Award. He has received fellowships from the Poetry Foundation, the McKnight Foundation, and the NEA and is a member of the Dark Noise Collective.

ELIZABETH SPENCER SPRAGINS is a writer, poet, and editor who taught in community colleges for more than a decade. Her tanka and bardic verse in the Celtic style have been published in England, Scotland, Canada, Indonesia, and the United States. Recent work has appeared in the *Quarterday Review*, *The Lyric*, *Glass: Facets of Poetry*, *Halcyon Days*, and *Peacock Journal*. She lives in Fredericksburg, Virginia.

GERALD STERN is the author of twenty books of poetry, including *This Time: New and Selected Poems*, for which he received the National Book Award in 1998, and *Leaving Another Kingdom: Selected Poems*. His most recent books of poems are *Galaxy Love*, *Divine Nothingness*, and *In Beauty Bright*.

ANITA SULLIVAN helped found Oregon's only poetry publishing collective, Airlie Press. She has a recent poetry chapbook, *And If the Dead Do Dream*, and an essay collection, *The Bird That Swallowed the Music Box*, is forthcoming from Shanti Arts Press.

WISŁAWA SZYMBORSKA (1923–2012), a Polish poet who won the Nobel Prize for Literature in 1996, was also an essayist and translator. Her poems, marked by irony, plain language, and sometimes wry humor, deal with both trivial subjects as well as the large subjects of war and terrorism. Her books include *The End and the Beginning*, *View with a Grain of Sand*, and *Miracle Fair: Selected Poems*.

ADAM TAVEL won the 2017 Richard Wilbur Book Award for *Catafalque* (University of Evansville Press, 2018). He is also the author of *The Fawn Abyss* (Salmon Poetry, 2017) and *Plash & Levitation* (University of Alaska Press, 2015), which won the Permafrost Book Prize.

SUSAN TERRIS's most recent books are *Take Two: Film Studies* and *Memos*, both from Omnidawn Publishing, and *Ghost of Yesterday: New & Selected Poems* (Marsh Hawk Press). She has published widely in literary journals, and her work has appeared in Pushcart Prize XXXI and *Best American Poetry 2015*. She is currently a poetry editor of *Pedestal Magazine*.

SHU TING is the pen name of the Chinese woman poet Gōng Pèiyú, a member of the twentieth-century Misty Poets group, whose work was considered obscure (therefore "misty") and also in opposition to the poetic standards of the Cultural Revolution. She is the author of two collections of poetry: *The Mist of My Heart: Selected Poems of Shu Ting* and *Shu Ting: Selected Poems*.

TOMAS TRANSTRÖMER (1931–2015), a Swedish poet and writer, was awarded the Nobel Prize in Literature in 2011. His many books of poems, translated into English, include *Truth Barriers*, *The Half-Finished Heaven*, *Selected Poems 1954–1986*, *The Great Enigma: New Collected Poems*, and *For the Living and the Dead*.

TU FU (712–70), who wrote during the Tang Dynasty, is considered one of the greatest Chinese poets. He lived during a time of political unrest, and many of his poems are concerned with war and suffering. But he also wrote about domestic life, art, and animals, among other common topics. Zhang Jie, a twentieth-century Chinese novelist, has written that for Tu Fu, "everything in this world is poetry."

TIM VINCENT teaches writing and literature at Duquesne University in Pittsburgh, Pennsylvania. His poems have recently appeared in anthologies from Concrete Wolf Press and Grayson Books. He is a 2016 and 2017 winner in the GRSF/Maria W. Faust Sonnet Contest.

VIRGIL is considered to be the greatest Roman poet of antiquity. His epic poem, the *Aeneid* (c. 30 BCE), recounts the legend of Aeneas, a Trojan soldier who left that fallen city and traveled to Italy, where he founded the city of Rome.

OCEAN VUONG's first poetry collection, *Night Sky with Exit Wounds*, was a *New York Times* Top 10 Book of 2016. The winner of the T. S. Eliot Prize, a Whiting Award, a Thom Gunn Award, and the Forward Prize for Best First Collection, Vuong's honors include fellowships from the Lannan Foundation and the Academy of American Poets.

BONNIE RAE WALKER's poetry has been published in journals such as *Red Paint Hill Poetry Journal*, *San Pedro River Review*, *Steel Toe Review*, *Whale Road Review*, and more. She lives in San Diego.

WALT WHITMAN (1819–92), arguably the most important American poet along with Emily Dickinson, has been called the father of free verse. His poetry, marked by its humanist stance toward the world, embodies elements of both transcendentalism and realism. His major work, an epic poem called *Leaves of Grass*, was self-published in 1855, but he continued to revise and expand it until his death in 1892.

WILLIAM CARLOS WILLIAMS (1883–1963) was a medical doctor and a poet whose work was initially linked to the Imagist movement of Ezra Pound, though later he embraced a modernist free verse that favored colloquial language and distinctly personal subject matter. His most famous books are *Spring and All* and his epic poem of place, *Paterson*.

CHARLES WRIGHT has published numerous books of poetry, including *Country Music: Selected Early Poems*, which won the Pulitzer Prize in 1983; *Negative Blue*; *Appalachia*; and *Black Zodiac*, which won the Pulitzer Prize and the Lenore Marshall Poetry Prize from the American Academy of Poets. His many honors include the Ruth Lilly Poetry Prize. In 2014, he was named poet laureate of the United States.

Joseph Zaccardi served as the Marin County, California, poet laureate from 2013 to 2015. During his tenure, he edited *Changing Harm to Harmony: Bullies & Bystanders Project*. His fourth collection of poems, *A Wolf Stands Alone in Water,* was published by CW Books in 2015.

Matthew Zapruder is the author of four books of poetry, most recently *Sun Bear* and *Come On All You Ghosts,* as well as a book of prose, *Why Poetry.* He is an associate professor in the graduate program at St. Mary's College of California and an editor-at-large at Wave Books. In 2016–17, he held the annually rotating position of editor of the Poetry Column for *The New York Times Magazine.*

Permissions

We gratefully acknowledge permission to reprint the following copyrighted works:

Elizabeth Alexander, "One week later in the strange," from *Crave Radiance: New and Selected Poems 1990-2010* by Elizabeth Alexander (Graywolf Press, 2010). Used by permission.

Dante Alighieri, excerpt from *Paradiso*, translated by Robert and Jean Hollander. Translation copyright © 2007 by Robert Hollander and Jean Hollander. Used by permission of Doubleday, an imprint of the Knopf Doubleday Publishing Group, a division of Penguin Random House LLC. All rights reserved.

Rick Barot, "Coast Starlight," from *Chord* by Rick Barot (Louisville: Sarabande Books, 2015). Used by permission of Sarabande Books, Inc.

Ellen Bass, "Ode to the Heart," from *Like a Beggar* by Ellen Bass (Copper Canyon Press, 2014). Used by permission of Copper Canyon Press.

Bei Dao, "The Morning's Story," translated by Bonnie S. McDougal and Chen Maipeng, from *Old Snow*, © 1991 by Bei Dao. Translation © 1991 by Bonnie S. McDougall and Chen Maiping. Reprinted by permission of New Directions Publishing Corp.

Michael Benedikt, "The Thermometer and the Future," from *Night Cries*. Copyright © 1976 by Michael Benedikt. Reprinted by permission of the Estate of Michael Benedikt.

Joshua Bennett, "America Will Be," published in *The Nation*, January 1, 2018. © Joshua Bennett. Used by permission of the author. Reprinted here in a slightly different form.

Reginald Dwayne Betts, "When I Think of Tamir Rice While Driving," appeared in an earlier form in *Poetry*, April 2016. Copyright © 2018 Reginald Dwayne Betts. Used by   permission of the author.

Frank Bidart, "Mourning What We Thought We Were," from *The New Yorker* (January 23, 2017). Reprinted with permission of the author.

Chana Bloch, "Death March, 1945," from *Swimming in the Rain* by Chana Bloch (Autumn House Press, 2015). Used by permission of Autumn House Press.

Jericho Brown, "The Tradition," from *Poem-a-Day* (online), August 7, 2015. Used by permission of the author.

C. P. Cavafy, "The City," from *C. P. Cavafy: Collected Poems*, translated by Edmund Keeley and Philip Sherrard. Copyright © 1992 by Edmund Keeley and Philip Sherrard. Reprinted by permission of Princeton University Press.

Lucille Clifton, "won't you celebrate with me," from *The Book of Light* (Copper Canyon Press, 1993). Used by permission of Copper Canyon Press.

Laura Da', "American Towns," from *Tributaries* by Laura Da'. Copyright © 2015 Laura Da'. Reprinted by permission of the University of Arizona Press.

Mahmoud Darwish, "Another Damascus in Damascus," from *Unfortunately, It Was Paradise* by Mahmoud Darwish, translated and edited by Munir Akash and Carolyn Forche. Copyright © 2002, 2013 by The Regents of the University of California. Reprinted by permission of the University of California Press.

Mai Der Vang, "Dear Exile," from *Afterland* by Mai Der Vang (Graywolf Press, 2017). Used by permission.

Natalie Diaz, "Why I Don't Mention Flowers When Conversations with My Brother Reach Uncomfortable Silences," from *When My Brother Was an Aztec* (Copper Canyon Press, 2012). Used by permission of Copper Canyon Press.

Emily Dickinson, "These Strangers, in a foreign World," from *The Poems of Emily Dickinson*, edited by Thomas H. Johnson, Cambridge, Mass.: The Belknap Press of Harvard University Press, Copyright © 1951, 1955 by the President and Fellows of Harvard College. Copyright © renewed 1979, 1983 by the President and Fellows of Harvard College. Copyright © 1914, 1918, 1919, 1924, 1929, 1930, 1932, 1935, 1937, 1942, by Martha Dickinson Bianchi. Copyright © 1952, 1957, 1958, 1963, 1965, by Mary L. Hampson. Used by permission.

Camille T. Dungy, "What I know I cannot say," from *Trophic Cascade* by Camille T. Dungy, copyright © 2017 by Camille T. Dungy. Published by Wesleyan University Press. Used by permission.

Molly Giles, "Letter to My Country in War Time," originally published in *The Rise Up Review*, May 2016. Reprinted with permssion of the author.

Miriam Bird Greenberg, "Spirit Level," from *In the Volcano's Mouth* by Miriam Bird Greenberg. Copyright 2016. Reprinted by permission of the University of Pittsburgh Press.

Susan Griffin, "Song," from *Dear Sky* by Susan Griffin (Shameless Hussy Press, 1971). Copyright © Susan Griffin. Used by permission of the author.

Robert Hass, "Winged and Acid Dark," from *Time and Materials: Poems 1997–2005* by Robert Hass. Copyright © 2007 by Robert Hass. Reprinted by permission of HarperCollins Publishers.

Robert Hayden, "Frederick Douglass," from *The Collected Poems of Robert Hayden* by Robert Hayden, edited by Frederick Glaysher. Copyright © 1966 by Robert Hayden. Used by permission of Liveright Publishing Corporation.

Terrance Hayes, "American Sonnet for My Past and Future Assassin," in *American Poetry Review*, July/August 2017. Copyright © by Terrance Hayes. Used by permission of author.

Seamus Heaney, "From the Republic of Conscience," from *Opened Ground: Selected Poems 1966–1996* by Seamus Heaney. Copyright © 1998 by Seamus Heaney. Reprinted by permission of Farrar, Straus & Giroux.

Juan Felipe Herrera, "War Voyeurs," from *Half of the World in Light: New and Selected Poems* by Juan Felipe Herrera (University of Arizona Press, 2008). Reprinted with permission of the author.

Brenda Hillman, "Short Anthem for the General Strike," from *Seasonal Works with Letters on Fire*, copyright © 2013 by Brenda Hillman. Published by Wesleyan University Press. Used by permission.

Tony Hoagland, "Gorgon," appeared online in an earlier form at *Love's Executive Order*, 2016. Used by permission of the author.

Robinson Jeffers, "Shine, Perishing Republic," copyright © 1934 by Robinson Jeffers & renewed 1962 by Donnan Jeffers and Garth Jeffers; from *The Selected Poetry of Robinson Jeffers*. Used by permission of Random House, an imprint and division of Penguin Random House LLC. All rights reserved.

Tyehimba Jess, "Jubilee Blues," from *Olio* (Seattle: Wave Books, 2016). Used by permission of Wave Books.

Jaan Kaplinski, "The East-West border . . . ," translated by the author with Sam Hamill and Riina Tamm, from *The Wandering Border* (Copper Canyon Press, 1987). Used by permission of Copper Canyon Press.

Yusef Komunyakaa, "Thanks," from *Dien Cai Dau*, copyright © 1988 by Yusef Komunyakaa. Published by Wesleyan University Press. Used by permission.

Virgil, "The Departure from Fallen Troy," lines 692–719, from the *Aeneid*, translated by David Ferry, in *Bewilderment, New Poems and Translations* by David Ferry (University of Chicago Press, 2012). Used by permission.

Ocean Vuong, "Aubade with Burning City," from *Night Sky with Exit Wounds* (Copper Canyon Press, 2016). Used by permission of Copper Canyon Press.

Charles Wright, "Sunlight Bets on the Come," from *Bye-and-Bye: Selected Late Poems* by Charles Wright. Copyright © 2011 by Charles Wright. Used by permission of Farrar, Straus & Giroux.

Matthew Zapruder, "Sun Bear," from *Sun Bear* (Copper Canyon Press, 2014). Used by permission of Copper Canyon Press.

Index of First Lines

A mother and the son   *47*

A new country is formed   *12*

A sentence with "dappled shadow" in it.   *51*

A single porch light burns in the flooded trailer park   *149*

A word has abolished another word   *151*

After every war   *57*

All I hear in the U.S. is U.   *56*

America, I do not call your name without hope   *154*

An old, mad, blind, despised, and dying king;   *150*

"And thus, as harmony's sweet sound may rise   *112*

Another Damascus in Damascus, an eternal one.   *118*

As a way of approaching a river; a kind of gill net.   *21*

As he spoke we could hear, ever more loudly, the noise   *106*

Aster. Nasturtium. Delphinium. We thought   *165*

At Auction Negro Man in Loincloth   *79*

Back again . . . *talkin' about heaven* . . . No blood, no pus . . .   *127*

because white men can't   *67*

By the turn of the century   *125*

Caligula, son of Germanicus, gave the people   *128*

Did Noah ask God, as they walked together, what about   *152*

Even though we watch every year   *99*

Everywhere I go, people are shouting   *26*

Farouk lifted the old Cadillac up onto 80 going west   *116*

for the joke, even the pun,   *96*

God did not lead us by the nearer way   *144*

Having helped initiate   *139*

He said: "It was a country then."   *110*

He who ordered the death   *15*

Human reason is beautiful and invincible.   *157*

I am now at the age where my father calles me brother   *168*

I am of old and young, of the foolish as much as the wise,   *140*

I did but prompt the age to quit their clogs   *8*

I do not understand why men make war.   *37*

I like it when we sit in the backyard   *145*

I play Haydn after a black day   *170*

I read to the entire plebe class,   *22*

I tried to put a bird in a cage.   *91*

I turn my back as winter sun sets   *14*

I wander thro' each charter'd street,   *124*

I watched history unfold today.   *166*

If we must have violence, then let it be   *63*

I'm worried about truth, that it's a hunger . . .   27

In all these rotten shops, in all this broken furniture   62

In that tenth winter of your exile   89

in the backseat, my sons laugh & tussle,   70

In the basin, the sun sears fabric   34

In the beginning the powder was without   48

In the beginning, we wept.   6

In the front hallway   46

In the Kashmir mountains,   52

It is never admitting you've been to a bullfight.   117

It was difficult to connect the dots.   167

It's cold, and my son is small.   163

It's late in the day and the old school's deserted   143

i've left Earth in search of darker planets, . . .   68

Let them not say: we did not see it.   174

Like the topaz in the toad's head   130

Lord, don't let us give over our daughters   158

Milkflower petals on the street   42

My daughter's gone to march with her troop   146

My father once filmed a stop-action scene   28

My Portion is Defeat—today—   29

Never step back   Never a last   107

Not like the brazen giant of Greek fame,   113

Now that you need your prescription glasses to see the stars   160

Oh God, she said   40

Once burst loose from human bondage,   82

One week later in the strange   142

Out of the station. Out of the rail-yard's braiding   131

Perhaps our hearts   23

Plentiful sacrifice and believers in redemption   133

Prepare your baggage   111

proves elusive and reluctant to speak but agrees to man up   13

Reading the word *inauguration* for the hundredth time   147

Rilke ends his sonnet "Archaic Torso of Apollo" saying   76

saw grunts cut off Charlie's ear to confirm a kill   39

Seneca, Missouri—soft wash of casino jangle   59

She crouches near the East River   132

She looks at belts differently now   54

Snows heavy at Hsan-yang this tenth-year winter,   88

So that the truant boy may go steady with the State,   164

Someone had the idea of getting more water   123

Thanks for the tree   44

The alphabet keepers have delivered. In numerical order.   50

The basic pleasures remain unchanged,   172

The chickens   135

The East-West border is always wandering,   115

The forecast that morning said possible rain,   148

The laughter of women sets fire   173

The right of the strong is to take everything.   93

The serpent comes.   95

The shadow I had carried lightly has   80

The ship that took my mother to Ellis Island   108

The sky is always dark blue, trending toward lavender   87

The stream swirls. The wind moans in   136

The suffocating cockatoo falls limp   90

The truth is, I've never cared for the National   4

The unborn are giving speeches   5

"There was a muddy ditch at the side of the road   162

There's a place between two stands of trees where the grass grows uphill   3

These Strangers, in a foreign World,   105

They've sunk the posts deep into the ground,   114

This cold is awful, how did the temperature get down there so low? . . .   161

This morning I see that 100 men in suits . . .   92

To begin: 77

Truth has gone, like Thoreau,   94

Turning and turning in the widening gyre   134

Wandering around the Albuquerque Airport Terminal, after learning   24

We sailed to Angel Island, and for several hours   10

We were born into an amazing experiment.   19

We'll visit Caliban, my slave, who never   78

We're mashing up the believable and the inconceivable,   129

When a man is held at the airport   119

When I landed in the republic of conscience   34

When it is finally ours, this freedom, this liberty, this beautiful   83

When she casts herself as Antigone,   9

When they were called to the table,   30

When those radiant mango-eyed beings   171

When you shouted *there it is!*—   16

While this America settles in the mould of its vulgarity, heavily   98

won't you celebrate with me   141

yesterday at the Oakland zoo   100

you are my shelter from the storm   74

You said: "I'll go to another country, go to another shore,   97

You were invisible to me.   75

You were telling the story, and suddenly   73

Your knives tip down   81

Author Index

Abdo, Diya 110

Akers, Ellery 92

Alcantara, Jose A. 63

Alexander, Elizabeth 142

Alighieri, Dante 112

Anonymous 114

Barot, Rick 131

Bass, Ellen 143

Beckman, David 13

Bei Dao 151

Bellm, Dan 144

Benedikt, Michael 161

Bennett, Joshua 168

Betts, Reginald Dwayne 70

Bidart, Frank 19

Blake, William 124

Bloch, Chana 162

Bourbeau, Heather 14

Brown, Jericho 165

Casey-Whiteman, Jocelyn 167

Cavafy, C. P. 97

Centolella, Thomas 129

Clifton, Lucille 141

Cohen, Susan 16

Da', Laura 59

Daly, Matt 26

Daly, Patrick 152

Darwish, Mahmoud 118

Day, Lucille Lang 148

Der Vang, Mai 107

DeVilbiss, Ann 77

Di Stefano, Dante 158

Diaz, Natalie 52

Dickinson, Emily 105

Dine, Carol 46

Duncan, Susan G. 132

Dungy, Camille T. 10

Elliott, Chiyuma 21

Fisk, Molly 99

Fueston, Jen Stewart 163

Giles, Molly 56

Greenberg, Miriam Bird 12

Griffin, Susan 40

Halebsky, Judy 27

Hamer, Forrest 73

Hass, Robert 51

Hayden, Robert 83

Hayes, Terrance 76

Heaney, Seamus 32

Herrera, Juan Felipe 37

Hillman, Brenda 5

Hirshfield, Jane 174

Hoagland, Tony 160

Jeffers, Robinson 98

Jennings, Janet 128

Jess, Tyehimba 82

Kaplinski, Jaan 115

Komunyakaa, Yusef 44

Koster, Dana 48

Lang, Susanna 119

Lazarus, Emma 113

Le Guin, Ursula K. 130

Levine, Julia B. 149

Levine, Philip 108

Levis, Larry 164

Lewis, Robin Coste 79

Limón, Ada 4

Lorde, Audre 133

Luterman, Alison 6

Matthews, William 22

McCrae, Shane 80

McGuire, Dawn 54

McNally, Grace 9

Mead, Jane 123

Merwin, W. S. 89

Milosz, Czeslaw 157

Millson, Jack 166

Milton, John 8

Mueller, Lisel 173

Natchez, Meryl 96

Nathan, Leonard 15

Neruda, Pablo 30

Newman, Gail 94

Nye, Naomi Shihab 24

Olds, Sharon 75

Ott, Martin 28

Perreault, George 146

Pineda, Irma 111

Po Chü-i 88

Pryputniewicz, Tania 29

Rader, Dean 154

Rankine, Claudia 67

Rector, Liam 125

Rich, Adrienne 3

Rubio-Goldsmith, Christopher 117

Russell, Martin 47

Ryan, Kay 135

Šalamun, Tomaž 93

Schain, Eliot 116

Scott, Peter Dale 139

Sereno, Prartho 171

Sfeir, Mona Nicole 50

Shakespeare, William 78

Sharif, Solmaz 81

Shelley, Percy Bysshe 150

Shockley, Evie 74

Shu Ting 23

Smith, Austin 147

Smith, Danez 68

Spragins, Elizabeth Spencer 95

Stern, Gerald 62

Sullivan, Anita 87

Szymborska, Wisława 57

Tavel, Adam 90

Terris, Susan 127

Transt, Tomas 170

Tu Fu 136

Vincent, Tim 145

Virgil 106

Vuong, Ocean 42

Walker, Bonnie Rae 34

Whitman, Walt 140

Williams, William Carlos 91

Wright, Charles *172*
Yeats, William Butler *134*
Zaccardi, Joseph *39*
Zapruder, Matthew *100*

Sixteen Rivers Press is a shared-work, nonprofit poetry collective dedicated to providing an alternative publishing avenue for San Francisco Bay Area poets. Founded in 1999 by seven writers, the press is named for the sixteen rivers that flow into San Francisco Bay.

SAN JOAQUIN • FRESNO • CHOWCHILLA • MERCED • TUOLUMNE
STANISLAUS • CALAVERAS • BEAR • MOKELUMNE • COSUMNES
AMERICAN • YUBA • FEATHER • SACRAMENTO • NAPA • PETALUMA